IAIN MACINTO[SH]

EVERYTHING
YOU EVER WANTED
TO KNOW ABOUT
Rugby

(BUT WERE TOO AFRAID TO ASK)

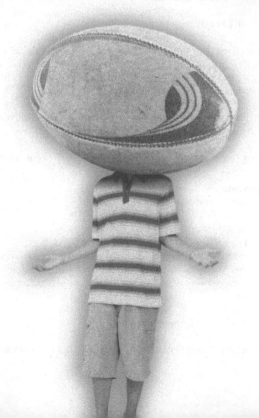

Note
Whilst every effort has been made to ensure that the content of this book
is as technically accurate and as sound as possible, neither the author nor the
publishers can accept responsibility for any injury or loss sustained as a result
of the use of this material.

First published 2010

Bloomsbury Publishing Plc
50 Bedford Square
London WC1B 3DP
www.bloomsbury.com

Reprinted 2013, 2014, 2015

Copyright © 2010, 2013 Iain Macintosh

ISBN 978 1 4081 1494 0

A CIP catalogue record for this book is available from the British Library.

Acknowledgements
Cover photograph © shutterstock.com
Illustrations by kja-artists
Designed by James Watson

This book is produced using paper that is made from wood grown in managed,
sustainable forests. It is natural, renewable and recyclable. The logging and
manufacturing processes conform to the environmental regulations of the
country of origin.

Typeset in Giovanni Book by seagulls.net

Printed and bound in Great Britain by CPI Group (UK) Ltd, Croydon CR0 4YY

Contents

Acknowledgements

This book is dedicated to my incredible wife Rachael whose love and support I really don't deserve. I must have done something pretty amazing in a previous life to land her and we're talking, like, really amazing. Rescuing 27 orphans from a flood or inventing fire, something like that.

My parents and my sister Isla were also hugely supportive throughout all of this and I can't begin to thank them enough. Of all the books I've written, this was by far the most difficult, but they were always there to help and advise. My dad, in particular, had to put up with a string of desperate phonecalls begging for counsel.

Matt Gallagher's patience and wisdom were vital throughout the process, my uncle Andrew Macintosh, a fount of knowledge on all things egg-shaped, came to my aid on more than one occasion and equally invaluable was the sage advice of Dan Bourke, Tom Riddle and Giles Daniels.

Charlotte Atyeo gave me this opportunity, for which I am incredibly grateful, while Lucy Beevor worked tirelessly to remove all the spelling mistakes, for which I am incredibly sorry.

Thanks also to the closet rugby fans on Southend United fan-site Shrimperzone.com, that's Shrimper, Uxbridge Shrimper, Alexis SUFC, Southchurch Groyney, Matt the Shrimp, Dashman, Libertine, Balmain Shrimper, Yorkshire Blue, Surrey Shrimper and Number 11.

Thanks also to Tony Pearson, Toby Fuhrman, Tom Warren, Shaun Nickless, James Findlay, Penny Rance, Dave Adams, Phil Adams, Mikey Grady, Nick Tate and everyone at The Endeavour Pub in Chelmsford.

Thanks to Steve Brierley for picking up on a number of truly horrifying grammatical errors in the final draft.

Author's note

As this book is written with the primary aim of telling people how mind-bogglingly wonderful rugby union is without baffling them with jargon, you'll have to forgive me always referring to the players as 'he'. I know that I shouldn't do it, but I feared that if every hypothetical situation became 'and then he/she will pass the ball out to his/her team-mate', it would swiftly become a nightmare.

Rugby is, of course, open to women as well and the level of their game, and the interest in it, is improving all the time.

Throughout the book 'rugby' will refer to rugby union, and not rugby league, unless otherwise stated.

Anyway, what are you doing still reading this? There's a beautiful game to discover.

Iain Macintosh

Why you should like rugby

'Any sport played with a ball that is shaped like an egg can only ever be inherently random.'

I used to say this rather a lot when I was younger. As a devout football fan, my rabid hatred of rugby was well known among my friends and family. I saw it as a game for public schoolboys, an unsophisticated and unlovable mess of bruised limbs and swollen ears. Where was the finesse of football? Where were the moments of genius that lift you from your seat? I might have felt differently, however, had I actually bothered to learn a bit about the game.

My first experience of rugby was, like most men's, entirely against my will. As a pitifully skinny eleven-year-old in his first year at comprehensive school, I was led out on to a quagmire of a pitch and, without even a cursory guide to the laws of the game, a ball was thrown, a whistle blew and the biggest boy in the class jumped on my head. I decided there and then, as I vainly searched for feeling in my legs, that I wanted nothing to do with this so-called sport.

A succession of kindly friends and relatives tried to cure me of my prejudices, but it wasn't until I approached adulthood that it all started to click. You see, something is always happening on a rugby pitch. There *are* moments of genius, there *is* finesse, you just need to banish the nightmares of comprehensive school and know what you're looking for.

The atmosphere at a rugby match is completely different from any other sport. It's boisterous, but it's friendly. There's banter, but it's benign. There's a deep understanding of the game because most fans have played it at one level or another.

In 2007, I wrote a book about football that involved a great deal of travelling, especially in taxis. Almost every driver, on finding out that I was a football writer, said the same thing.

'Football writer, eh? I used to love football, but it's not the same game now, is it? Too much money. You can't relate to teenage millionaires, it costs the best part of a week's wages to take the kids and that's only if you can get the tickets. Besides, they've taken out all the tackling. It's not really a man's game anymore.'

The sport that they were looking for, the entertaining, affordable, honourable game that they mourn, is in perfect health. It's just that these days we call it rugby. No bling-encrusted millionaires, no ludicrously expensive season tickets. Just unadulterated sport.

Rugby, at least at club level, is a physically democratic game. While other sports tend to be geared to only the tall or the lithe, there is a place on the rugby pitch for pretty much every body-shape. Are you as wide as you are tall? Wonderful, there's a place for you in the scrum. Do you have both the pace and the build of a whippet? Then you'll be welcome on the wings. But it isn't just a game for the players.

Watching rugby can be a glorious experience. At its best, the game is an astonishing spectacle to behold. It has been described by some as being rather like watching a war, which isn't strictly true of course, as people are very rarely killed and no government has ever had to concoct a pack of lies to start a rugby match. But the strategic intricacies and the close-up blood and thunder make the analogy worth pursuing.

It requires bravery, but not foolishness, and not only composure and common sense, but also the willingness to step out into the firing line. It is not a game for the timid.

The ex-England player Brian Moore, perhaps unwittingly, captured the ethos of rugby perfectly in a training video for the BBC's Sport Academy website. Using a young team of rugby players to demonstrate the finer points of the game, Moore proceeded to show how it was possible to unbalance a scrum by the position of your elbows at the bind, something which you'll find out all about later.

'What I'm trying to do,' grunted Moore from the inside of a worried-looking scrum, 'is put the loosehead prop in a really difficult position, because if he wants to lift up here, he'll have to do it when he's bent and twisted.'

'But ... erm ... is that not illegal?' asked Jeremy Guscott nervously.

'It's totally illegal,' confirmed Moore happily, 'but it's very effective!'

And that takes care of the one remaining obstacle to the enjoyment of rugby: the laws. Rugby is cursed with an ever-evolving law book, already too heavy for its own good, but as Moore so charmingly displayed, the laws are not integral to the understanding of the game. In fact, most rugby fans are still ignorant of many of them.

This book will make no effort to explain all of them, for there are far more comprehensive tomes on the market for that purpose. Instead, it is an attempt to demystify the game for anyone who has ever considered the possibility that it might be worth a look, but has been beaten back by an ignorance of the basics.

Here you will be given a crash course in how the game works, why it works and, perhaps most importantly, what you need to know to sit in a pub and get happily bladdered with complete strangers, roaring your approval at a maelstrom of muddy men. Rugby is a game that welcomes newcomers with open arms, even if those arms can occasionally be wrapped around your kneecaps. Come join me.

Crouch … touch … engage.

The history of rugby

Rugby, like Association Football, evolved from the mangled remnants of the traditional village football games of the Middle Ages. For centuries, the greatest form of organised leisure in the UK was for the entire community to wage open warfare over a pig's bladder filled with sawdust, battling like animals in the dirt for supremacy. The rules were vague at best and the violence was widespread. With the exception of murdering your opponent, which was still very much frowned upon, you could get away with almost anything. Indeed, if you're unfortunate enough to find yourself in the front row of a scrum today, you'll find that this is an aspect of the game that has been well preserved.

There was no single, official version of this primitive football. The rules, such as they were, differed from region to region. Most of them shared the aim of getting a ball from one marker to another, but some included goalposts for the ball to be kicked through, under or over. Some games allowed the use of hands, others just the feet. All were repeatedly banned by a succession of monarchs, although the people rarely paid attention to things like that, some of them going so far as to arrange secret games as a means of political dissent.

As industrialisation spread across Britain, these playful outpourings of competitive bottom-kicking and eye-gouging began to fade out with the green belt. Towns and factories started popping up and life in the inner cities became rather more regimented. Oddly, it was the public school system that stepped up to revive the game of the commoners.

As anyone who has ever raised a son to adulthood will know, adolescent boys are a bubbling cauldron of hormones. Wracked by a heady brew of new and conflicting chemicals, the sweet and tender young cherubs metamorphose into raging, spotty dervishes with far too much energy and bum-fluff moustaches. Putting hundreds of them into an enclosed space like a public school and reading Latin to them for hours on end was, in retrospect, a bad idea. Posh fee-paying schools in the 19th century were beset with civil disorder as pimply students went completely loco and started taking over the classrooms by force, seizing control of entire wings of the buildings. Some riots got so out of hand that soldiers were forced to enter the schools to quell the resistance.

Eventually some enterprising teachers, young enough to remember what it was like to be a teenager, figured out the cause of the restlessness and scheduled physical training sessions to work the aggression out of their pupils' systems. It soon became apparent that organised team sports were a good way of developing character as well as fitness, and a new form of football began to develop amongst the cloisters, with an emphasis on kicking, both of the ball and of other players.

Rugby, we are meant to believe, might never have evolved had it not been for the blatant and unashamed cheating of one William Webb Ellis at Rugby School in 1823. The official story is that Webb Ellis picked up the ball and ran with it, sliding in to touch down the world's first try. Amazed at his derring-do, his schoolmasters realised that this was a game far superior to football and so the world was changed. This delightful tale is probably not true for two reasons: firstly, that an act of skulduggery like that would have been rewarded with a sound beating rather than with congratulations, and secondly, that there is no record of this actually happening.

An 1895 inquiry into the origins of rugby found no conclusive evidence of the incident, bar a few sketchy stories, none of which were first hand. The real Webb Ellis left school, played cricket at Cambridge and became a clergyman, dying in France in 1872, entirely unaware that he would be credited with the birth of a sport.

Regardless of his efforts, this proto-football spread across the public schools of the land, changing slightly as it went. But as anyone who has ever played a game of pool during Freshers' Week will know, regionalised rules can cause great confusion. What is acceptable in the south might be a sin in the north, and students struggled to organise games at university because every player had a different idea of what was supposed to be happening. By the 1860s, there was a desperate need to settle upon some universal rules and codify the game.

Two key factions had emerged. The first, the largest of the two, wanted to eliminate 'hacking' from the game entirely, arguing that working men, who really rather relied upon their legs, would not be able to play if it was maintained. There was also a strong feeling that carrying the ball should be eliminated, but on this concessions were offered. It was 'hacking' that caused the breakdown in talks. But how could this be a game for men, argued the smaller faction, if you weren't allowed to attack each other?

Blackheath, one of the most vociferous representatives at the final meeting, withdrew and, with the opposition crumbling, The Football Association was founded in 1863 entirely bereft of hacking and carrying. In 1871, the Rugby Football Union sprang into life, proving to be so attractive that Richmond, a Football Association club, broke ranks and joined in. Rugby had made its first step as an independent sport.

While Association Football quickly turned professional, rugby's powerbrokers dug their heels in to try to preserve their amateur status. Theirs was a game played primarily by gentlemen schooled at great expense, and these gentlemen were in no mood to relinquish their status at the top of the game. They had affairs off the pitch that demanded their attention and their view seemed to be that if other people, by which they meant the working class, were *paid* to play rugby full time, they would be able to practise more and then would very quickly become rather good at it. Soon there wouldn't be any room left at the top for a well-bred chap to kick another well-bred chap. And that wouldn't do at all.

Unsurprisingly, there were a number of players not so well off who begged to differ. Why should they play for nothing when so many people were paying to watch them? As rugby grew in popularity and fixtures were arranged around the country, it became more and more of a problem for people to play. Rugby's strict code of amateurism forbade the payment of wages, or even compensation for those who had taken time off work. In the north of the country, resentment and bitterness began to fester.

Finally, in 1895, there came the great schism, the split between the rugby powers that would never be mended. One group made up mainly of Yorkshire-based clubs separated and went professional. They would eventually be known as rugby league. The rest were content to maintain their amateur status and their sport became known as rugby union. In the interests of clarity, that is the last mention that rugby league will receive within these pages, which isn't to say that it's a lesser sport, merely that it will cause confusion. Maybe I'll do a book on that next year.

The ideology of amateurism would continue for another century. Although amateurism may have started out as an elitist ploy, it later became one of the central tenets of everything the sport stood for. Amateurism, according to its defenders, preserved the inherent goodness of sport. It was competition without the vulgarities of whopping great pay cheques and transfer fees that could fund hospital wings. Not that everyone agreed, obviously. You can't feed your kids on good intentions.

Rugby union was spread by clubs and national sides on tours across the world. If you could handle a long steamship journey, then New Zealand, Australia and South Africa could all be visited for a series of games over a period of several months, and vice versa. It was through touring that tactics were developed and mimicked and friendships were made. This is a tradition that continues even now, all the way down to local club level, although the motivation there is often primarily to nip over the channel and stock up on cheap booze and cigarettes.

In 1910, the French national team joined in with the four home nations – England, Scotland, Wales and Ireland –

to create the Five Nations tournament, a popular round-robin affair that continued throughout the century, with the exception of a period between 1933 and 1947, when the French were banned for toying with professionalism. The Five Nations became a closely contested, passionate battle for pride within the region, fought on an annual basis to the delight of swelling crowds.

Rugby union evolved slowly over the 20th century with only minor rule changes or point adjustments as it went. Outside of semi-regular tours and the shifting tussle for supremacy in the Five Nations, the international game was never contested on the same scale as it was in football, but that changed in 1987 with the first Rugby Union World Cup. Held in New Zealand and Australia, it was the first sign that the game was changing forever. If a global tournament could now be marketed like this, what hope was there for amateurism?

Two more World Cups would come and go before the game's powerbrokers would bow to the inevitable. In 1995, the International Rugby Board (IRB) declared the game officially 'open'. Players and coaches could finally be paid for their services. With the floodgates breached, rugby could finally make the most of its potential.

Since then, the Five Nations have become Six with the inclusion of Italy, the Tri Nations has given Australia, New Zealand and South Africa a regular chance to lock horns, and the club game has been dismantled and rebuilt for the modern age. There are leagues and continental competitions. There are televised games and recognisable faces and there is extensive media coverage. Rugby union is in the best shape of its life, which is very good timing on your part. You've joined at just the right moment.

However, it's not going to make much sense if you don't know the rules, is it? Let's have a look at the teams for starters, eh?

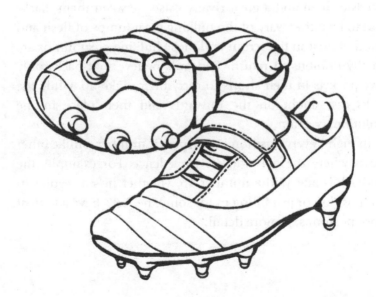

The basics

The players

There are fifteen players in a rugby team, divided into two groups: the forwards who contest the scrums and the backs who do most of the running. These are two very distinct breeds of men and a great rivalry exists between them. Backs tend to be rather wary of the hulking great lumps of flesh and hair that exist in the scrum and those hulking great lumps are equally dubious in return. Forwards believe that backs only have pockets in their shorts to carry their make-up, while the backs cast doubt on the forwards and their place in the evolutionary chain.

In rugby, every position has a specific number, unlike other sports where the player takes precedence. For example, the full-back is always the number 15, whether he's a regular in that position or just filling in for someone. Let's have a look at those positions in more detail.

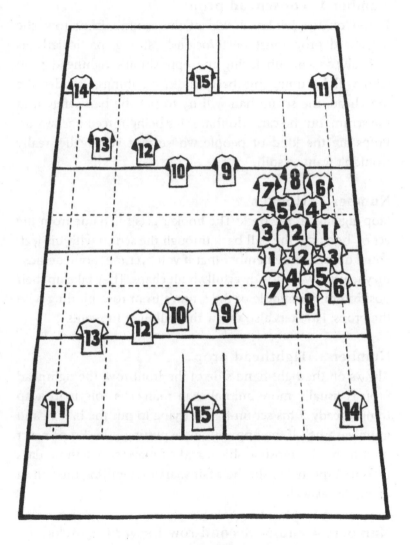

**The two teams of players lining up
at the start of a game**

Forwards

Number 1, Loosehead prop

Found on the left-hand side of the scrum's front row, the loosehead prop must be ferociously strong, particularly as he'll always end up facing the opposition's tighthead prop who will be doing his best to disrupt things. Besides the loosehead, the scrum-half will try to put the ball safely into the scrum, but he can't do that if it's being forced backwards. Props are the kind of people whose pint you really, really wouldn't want to spill.

Number 2, Hooker

Stop giggling at the back. The hooker gets his name from the act of 'hooking' the ball back through the scrum with his feet. You'll do well to remember that if you ever meet one because they're usually quite powerfully built chaps. They take up their position in the middle of the scrum's front row, binding with the props. Hookers also throw the ball in at line-outs.

Number 3, Tighthead prop

Always on the right-hand side of the front row, the tighthead prop is usually more animal than man. His role is to keep things steady if his scrum-half is trying to put the ball in and to unleash hell if the opposition are putting it in. Props never used to be the most sophisticated of players, but these days they are expected to do their fair share of handling the ball in open play as well.

Numbers 4 and 5, Second-row forwards (locks)

Behind the props and hooker, you'll find the second-row forwards, commonly known as 'locks'. Usually taller than the props, you can think of these boys as the engine room of the scrum, providing the power to drive the pack forwards. Their height also makes them the favoured targets in the line-out, where you may see them being lifted into the air by the props.

Number 6, Blindside flanker

Behind the second row is another row of three and, on the flank with the shortest distance to the sideline, you'll find the blindside flanker. As well as pushing the scrum, he will be integral to the defence and an occasional attacker. The play will usually gravitate to the widest part of the pitch, but every now and then a team might sneak up the blindside, and this chap's power will help.

Number 7, Openside flanker

When the ball comes out of the scrum and is distributed to the backs, it's usually only a matter of time before someone tackles them. When this 'breakdown' occurs, you need some muscle on the scene quickly and that's where the openside flanker comes in. He'll charge in and try to make sure that it is his team who win the resulting grapple for possession, or 'ruck' as it's known.

Number 8, Number eight

Surely they could have come up with a more imaginative name than this? It's a shame really, because the number eight is quite an important position. He's the only person, besides the scrum-half, who can pick up the ball at the back of a scrum and, although he'll usually get it to his team-mate as quickly as he can, sometimes a number eight will make a charge at the opposition and try to break their lines.

Backs

Number 9, Scrum-half

One of the most important players on the pitch, the scrum-half should be like the conductor of an orchestra. He tends to be small, quick and blessed with rat-like cunning because he'll want to wait for the right moment to start the ball moving along the back-line or direct play to the forwards, or to just go it alone. He is the link between the forwards and the backs.

Number 10, Fly-half

If the scrum-half is the conduit from the forwards, then the fly-half is the leader of the backs. Again, he'll be smaller and quicker, with a penchant for kicking. A good scrum-half will deliver the ball to the fly-half safely, giving him time to judge the best course of action, so he needs to be clever and clear of thought. He is usually the team's preferred kicker as well.

Number 11, Left-winger

The backs will be spread out in a sloping line behind the scrum and on the left, unsurprisingly, you'll find the left-winger. As a move progresses up the pitch, the ball will be passed along the back-line, usually ending up with this chap or his right-side equivalent. He needs to be incredibly quick to evade the attentions of the opposition team and he needs to be brave because he'll be the recipient of several 'last-ditch' tackles.

Number 12, Inside centre

Just inside the fly-half is the first of the two centres, the inside centre. He will usually be larger than the outside centre because he's expected to take hits on a more regular basis. A centre should have exceptional handling skills and should be capable of releasing a quick pass that goes directly where his team-mate expects. There's no room for butter-fingers here.

Number 13, Outside centre

The outside centre needs to have some pace, because he's going to be the one trying to run ahead of the winger in order to set him up for what should be the final pass. Timing is everything in this position. Release the ball to the winger too early and he'll get hit hard, you won't score and he'll never speak to you again. Do it too late and you'll get hit hard, you won't score and you may never speak again.

Number 14, Right-winger

Depending on which way the back-line slants, the winger will either be at the end of the line, or out on his own on the other side. This means that a certain awareness is required in case the play is switched from one flank to the other, and there is always the risk that the opposition will attack and leave you as one of the final lines of defence. Not quite the last one though.

Number 15, Full-back

That honour belongs to the full-back, a fine, spirited fellow who hangs back to guard the try-line, or 'goal-line' as it is also known. Brave and strong in the tackle, he also needs to be able to catch, especially if the ball has been kicked up so high that it comes down with snow on it. In modern rugby, he can even get forward and join the back-line on the attack, but he should never neglect his defensive duties.

Substitutes

Teams can use a limited selection of substitutes to replace tired, injured or otherwise useless players. However, with so many specialised positions, it's not always that easy to find an adequate replacement. Only two members of the front row can be substituted in a game, but another five from anywhere else can be hooked off by the manager. There are also blood substitutions, which are quite different. Any bleeders are ordered off double-quick and replaced by a temporary stand-in who won't make quite so much mess. These blood substitutes do not count as regular substitutes, so you can have as many as are necessary.

The points

So, let's get cracking. Rugby is played between two teams of those fifteen players on an area of grass similar in size to a football pitch. Unlike football, however, the goals are not quite at either end. They are placed a maximum of 22 metres inside of the touchlines at either end instead. That's so the players can run behind the try-line to score tries.

Matches last for 80 minutes, divided into two 40-minute halves, separated by a ten-minute break in the middle. Time can be added on at the referee's discretion if injuries have held up the game, but at international level the clock will be stopped for all stoppages. The game can only end when the ball is kicked out of play which means that, hypothetically, as long as the ball never went out of play it could go on forever..

Now, the more observant of you will already have noticed the goals and their very strange H-like quality. They are shaped like this because there are two basic ways to score points in rugby. One, as we've just touched on, is to evade the attentions of your opponents and to place the ball down beyond the goal-line to score a try. The other is to kick the ball over the crossbar and between the posts for a goal.

In the early days of rugby, no points were awarded for a try at all. Instead, the team that touched the ball down would just get a 'try' at kicking for a goal. Aha, see what they've done there? Remember that one, it's useful for impressing people in the pub with. It was only in later years, when the legislators realised that getting the ball down for a try was probably more difficult than merely tonking it over the crossbar, that the rules were changed and the points redistributed. These days, you get five points for a try and you still get the chance to kick a goal as well.

After a try, the ball is placed on the ground anywhere in line with where it was touched down and one player will run up and attempt to kick it between the posts. Positioning is very important, which is why you'll often see players running over the line and cutting in towards the goal before going down. That means that the kick will be taken from right in front of the posts. If they don't cut in, the kicker has to kick from a funny angle, lessening the chance of getting the ball on target. If the kick is good, two further points are added to the score (known as a 'conversion'). A central try should therefore, if the kicker is halfway competent, be worth seven points to the team, but one nearer the sidelines may prove too difficult and only deliver five.

In the general run of the game, known as 'open play', players can kick goals at any time. Mind you, that's easier said than done. Anything that goes over the crossbar and between the posts is worth three points. There are also penalties awarded for infringements and they can be kicked for three points as well. So if your team scored two tries, converted one of them, kicked a goal and scored three penalties, you would have?

That's right, 24 points. See? It's easy.

Passing

The crucial difference between rugby and any other sport is that the ball can only be passed backwards or sideways, never forwards. It can be thrown, hurled or lobbed, it can be dispatched all the way across the pitch from left to right, right to left, or just passed at close quarters from one player to another, but it must never go forwards. If a player unintentionally passes the ball forwards, a scrum is awarded to the opposing team. In the unlikely event that the player did it deliberately, a penalty would be awarded, but as this is one of the most fundamental rules in the game, it doesn't happen very often.

The man with the ball is vitally important to the understanding of the basic principles of the offside rule, which is fairly crucial as well. Any of his team-mates silly enough to stand in front of him while involving themselves in the game will be deemed offside and will be penalised. Unlike in football, you can't deploy players at the other end of the pitch and then just kick it all the way down to them. You actually have to work your way there on foot.

These two rules mean that most rugby matches, if viewed from above, would look a bit like two giant zigzags bouncing off each other, with the ball-carrier as the most advanced point and his team-mates fanning out behind him. It puts an emphasis on running with the ball and it makes rugby a game of territorial possession.

Not that this means you can't kick it forwards. In fact, one common tactic is to kick the ball hard along the ground into the opposition's half and then sprint after it, hoping to get there just as the opposing player picks it up, with hilarious or bone-crunching consequences. This is called a 'grubber kick' and, because of the shape of the ball, it causes a most irregular bounce. Imagine a rugby ball coming at you at speed, wobbling about and rearing up in the air unexpectedly. Now imagine fifteen big, hairy men sprinting 20 yards behind it, staring at you with a nasty glint in their eyes. Now try and catch the ball. Yikes.

However, the ball doesn't have to be kicked into the ground. By kicking it high into the air and chasing after it, it's possible to put the opposition under pressure. The defending player will have the chance to jump up and catch the ball unmolested, but he has to land at some point... This is called an 'up and under' or a 'Garryowen', after the Irish rugby club that popularised the tactic.

Of course, if you do keep kicking the ball, there's a strong chance that the other team are going to just keep it. Kicking is a really good way of losing possession, so the long kicks are more often used as a way of relieving pressure on the defence.

Anyway, those are the basics of the game outlined for you. We're now at the point where, if I were teaching you how to play cards, we'd have a couple of practice hands. In that spirit, let's conjure up a fictional rugby match and go through some of the things you are likely to see.

Passages of play and kick-off

Before a game of rugby can even begin, the two captains must first toss a coin and decide who will kick off. The winner of the toss can either choose to take the kick, or pick which end they will attack until half-time when they will have to swap round. On a windy or particularly sunny day, this can be a very important decision indeed.

The two teams then gather in their own halves and wait for the kicker to get the game underway by drop kicking the ball into the opposition's half. The kicker can opt either to hammer the ball towards the opposition goal-line, putting his adversaries as far away as possible from his own half, or to loop a short kick into the air. A shorter start will give his bigger players more of a chance of reaching the catcher before he has time to know what to do with the ball and it increases the pressure right from the start. That said, if he does catch it well and pass it quickly, you've just given possession away near the halfway line.

Is it better to push your opponents back, but give them the time to work up their momentum from their own goal-line, or is it more prudent to try and get stuck into their ranks before they settle? There's no right answer.

The ball has to travel at least 10 metres or the kicking team will be asked to take it again or, at the referee's discretion, a scrum will be awarded to the receiving team in the centre of the pitch. So there's nothing to be gained from just tapping it lightly into play.

Mind you, you can't welly it off the pitch either. If it goes straight out over the sidelines without touching the ground, the receiving team can take either a line-out or a scrum in the centre, or just ask for the ball to be kicked again. What about kicking it long behind the posts then? Nope, that's out as well. Anything that crosses the goal-line can potentially be grounded for a scrum in the centre or, again, another kick can be demanded. If it goes all the way past the dead-ball line, it's a 22-metre drop-out, something else you'll find out about later.

Receiving a kick is no fun at all. The ball could be wobbling in midair, the wind could take it out of position or the sun could blind you to its progress altogether. It takes a lot of skill to repeatedly take these catches and no small amount of intelligence to know what to do with one if you get it. One slip, one fumble, just one moment's hesitation will invite the intimate attentions of hundreds of kilograms of fast-moving bone and muscle.

The ruck

Now, let's imagine that you are the poor, wretched catcher, seconds away from collision with the opposition's most terrifying forward. You take the ball cleanly – we'll give you the dignity of doing that bit right – and, as you smile in satisfaction at a job well done, you get wiped out by 6 foot 5 inches of meat, teeth and body odour. After a 'tackle', as this near-death experience will be so underwhelmingly termed, both the tackler and the tacklee must relinquish the ball and, if possible, roll away. Of course, while you're desperately trying to wriggle to safety, everyone else is trying to get the ball and a ruck will develop above you. It may look like a comprehensive school lunch time bundle to you right now, but a ruck is one of the most important and oft-seen occurrences in the game of rugby.

Two of your team-mates in this example – for a ruck is anything with over three people – will clash for supremacy with two of your smelly assailant's friends by pushing at each other, trying to force the middle of this ruck over the grounded ball like an inverse game of tug-of-war. More and more players can join the ruck from either team, forcing and pushing but, and this is rather important, not touching the ball with their hands. That would be too easy. The players are encouraged to 'ruck' the ball out behind them with their feet and you're directly underneath them, so it could get a little painful. The team that successfully forces their opponents away will gain control of the ball and force it back to one of their team-mates, usually the little scrum-half, and the ball will be either sent off towards the backs or given short to the forwards. You, on the other hand, will be spitting dirt and studs and checking that all your facial features are still in the right place. Don't worry, though, as the referee is under strict instructions to keep a close eye on unnecessary violence. But he can't see everything...

Rucks are not always so closely contested. In fact, you'll often see players running directly into tackles and falling so that their body is in front of the ball, which can then be quickly retrieved by their team-mates. With strong enough forwards, it's a good way of trying to repeatedly smash holes in the defensive line. A well-drilled team will have the first wave of ruckers quickly on hand, bound together by their interlocking arms and pushing hard and low against their opponents. If you can be fairly sure that your team-mates will win their share of rucks, then you're not losing the ball, you're 'recycling' it.

Phases of play

This is probably a good place to describe 'phases of play', something you'll hear being mentioned quite a lot if you watch a televised game. When a player is tackled, which is known as 'the breakdown', it is the end of that phase of play. After the ensuing ruck or maul, it is a whole new phase of rugby. Teams who can retain possession of the ball after repeated breakdowns are playing 'phase rugby'.

Some teams, instead of retaining possession, have a tendency to boot the ball down the pitch, forcing the opposition onto the back foot, but losing control of the game in the process. It's primitive rugby and it doesn't make for entertaining viewing.

Phase rugby can help teams play to their strengths by pushing the game to the areas of the pitch where they can dominate. For example, a team with an excellent kicker might try and force the play to the centre of the pitch in order to attempt a drop goal. They would do this by making a series of probing runs towards the centre, making sure that the breakdown was always guarded by some hefty forwards, retaining the ball and making advances of several yards a phase until they entered the kicker's range. It's a lot easier to say than it is to do, especially as the opposition will know what you're up to and will hit you even harder to make sure that you stop it, but it's a common tactic all the same.

The maul

Right, let's get back to that game. You've picked yourself up off the ground, pulled the clump of wet mud out of your ear and noticed that your team won the ruck and are moving forwards up the pitch. Another breakdown results in another ruck, which your team wins and suddenly the ball is passed to you. You run forwards, because you're getting the hang of this now, but you're met by an opponent who tackles you hard, but not quite hard enough to knock you over. Still standing and still clutching the ball, you feel the wet thud of two of your team-mates who have come lolloping over to start pushing you forwards. Your opponents come in behind you and push back. You're now the meat in a rugby sandwich and, more importantly, this is a 'maul'.

The main difference between a maul and a ruck is that the player who has been tackled is on his feet, not on the ground. Your team-mates still gather behind you and the object is still to prevent the other team gaining control of the ball. However, the key benefit of a maul is that it can move forwards, all the way to the try-line in some cases, while the ball can be smuggled rearwards through the pack towards the safety of the second row. This is known as a 'driving maul'. It's particularly useful if the ball is in play quite close to the try-line and only a few more yards are needed before someone can touch the ball down and claim those five points.

But beware: the maul can only be maintained for as long as it is still moving. Once it stops, the referee will shout 'use it or lose it' and a decision must be made. Either the ball comes out towards the backs or it is shifted sideways – never forwards remember – to a new destination where a new maul can be

Author's note:

In 2008, the IRB began to experiment with a number of law changes, known as the Experimental Law Variations (ELVs). One of these alterations allowed opposing teams to pull mauls to the ground, which tended to stop them in their tracks rather quickly. As a result, the influence of the maul lessened dramatically. However, after fierce opposition from clubs, players and officials alike, the IRB dropped the alteration in 2009. Now mauling is back in fashion, and rightly so. Rugby has evolved over the past century and a half as a game of physical strength and exertion. To take out something as distinctive as a maul, or at least to allow an alteration to the laws that would make them far less effective, seems a little unfair.

formed. This is known as a 'rolling maul' and can leave the ball vulnerable to the opposition.

If the maul stops moving and nothing appears to be happening, the referee will award a scrum to the defending side. That's where the 'lose it' part of his slogan comes in, you see, and as I'm creating this hypothetical rugby match, that's what I've decided has just happened to you. It's a scrum, they've got the put-in and in about five minutes, you'll actually know what all of that means.

The scrum

The scrum is rugby union's way of restarting a game after an accidental infringement, or in some cases if the attacking team prefer, after a deliberate one. The culpable team will have to defend, while the other side get to put the ball in, or the 'put-in', as it is known. In this case, as it was your side who erred by not making use of that maul, this means that the opposing scrum-half will wait for the scrum to form and then, on the referee's command, will put the ball into the middle for his front-row forwards to, hopefully, win control of.

Now, you might want to take a quick look at those positional descriptions on page 19 again to remind yourself of who's who in the scrum. There should be, working left to right, a front row of the loosehead prop, the hooker and the tighthead prop. Behind them is the second row, made up of your two lock forwards, giants that they are. On the outside of the locks are those flankers, blindside on the flank with the shortest distance to the sideline, openside with the longest, and in between the flankers is the number eight. While the rest of the scrum can only hook the ball behind them with their feet, he's actually allowed to use his hands to pick it up and pass it to the scrum-half, who will have run round from the side and will be ready and waiting.

Your front row will be eager to make sure that none of that happens by pushing as hard as they can to gain control of the ball in order to hook it back to their own scrum-half. If that happens then the scrum will have 'gone against the head'. This doesn't happen very often, but when it does, the members of the scrum will brag about it for hours, like Viking warriors returning from a surprisingly unguarded coastline. Ordinarily, though, the ball is hooked backwards by the team with the put-in, through the scrum towards the rear where it can be distributed to the backs.

Scrums are very carefully monitored as they have the potential to go horribly wrong. With that much strength pushing and straining, accidents can happen. The referee will take every care to make sure that the scrum is constructed safely. He'll wait for the players to get into position and then shout 'crouch'. The players will drop to their haunches and he'll yell 'touch' to allow them to put their arms forwards and guide themselves in. You don't want to have your neck in the wrong place at a time like this. After inspecting the 'touch' of the scrum, usually after warning them to 'pause' first, he'll shout 'engage' and a scene reminiscent of those David Attenborough programmes on duelling stags will take its sweaty shape right before your eyes.

In this instance, the scrum goes well for your opponents, the ball is hooked back through the pack, delivered to the scrum-half who in turn passes to the fly-half and then … well, and then what? Your opponents are deep inside their own half, there's a long way to go before they'll score. What should they do? Why, they should kick for touch of course!

The kick for touch

If you have a look at the rugby pitch, you'll see that there is a big white line, 22 yards out from the try-line. With the same searing originality that was responsible for the name 'number eight' being given to the man in the number eight shirt, this line is called 'the 22-yard line' and it's very important. If the opposition have possession of the ball inside your 22, it's squeaky bottom time and no mistake.

If a defending team suddenly regains possession of the ball inside their own 22, however, you will almost certainly see them kicking the ball off the pitch as far away from their own goal-line as they can get it. This is 'kicking for touch' and it happens quite regularly in your average rugby match because it's a quick way of getting the ball to safety and clearing the lines. Some particularly plucky teams may occasionally try to pass the ball out of danger, but why bother? Rugby is a territorial game and if the ball is nowhere near your territory, you can't concede points.

When the ball goes out over the sidelines, a 'line-out' is awarded to the team who didn't touch it last, but we'll come to that in a minute. The most important thing here is where the line-out takes place. It may be rugby's version of the football 'throw-in', but it doesn't work in quite the same way. If the ball is kicked from outside the 22-yard line, the line-out isn't taken from where it leaves the field of play, rather it's taken from the sidelines adjacent to where it was kicked. Welly a ball up and off the pitch from 25 yards out and all you'll succeed in doing is giving the opposition a line-out, 25 yards from your goal-line.

Only if the ball is kicked from within that defensive 22-yard line does a line-out take place from where the ball leaves

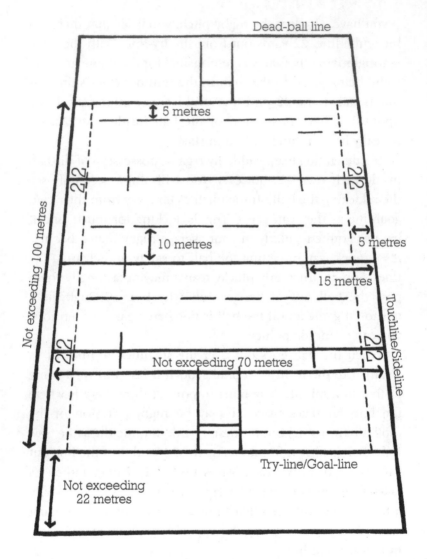

A typical rugby pitch

the pitch. However, that's not the case if the defending team gain control of the ball from outside of their 22 and then dart back in to make their kick, thus pushing the play all the way up the field. Cowardly tactics like that result in a line-out to the other team from where the ball was kicked, ensuring that no advantage is gained.

In our hypothetical game, with your team having won a couple of rucks and forcing the opposition back to within their 22 before a badly executed maul gave possession away, this is a perfect time for them to kick for touch. And they do so, thumping the ball out of their own half and straight off the pitch inside your half of the field. It's a line-out to your team, so let's find out how they work.

The line-out

Aesthetically, line-outs are wonderful things. Imagine two grizzly bears lifting an elephant above their shoulders while a gorilla throws a ball at them and you're pretty close, especially in terms of the shockwaves they'd create when they all hit the ground. Anyone silly enough to dismiss rugby as an 'ugly game' has obviously never seen one of these.

To restart the game when the ball has passed out of play on the flanks, the hooker will stand on the sidelines and throw it up in the air between two rows of opposing players. There must be a gap of 1 metre between the row and the ball must be thrown straight down the middle of it. So, if the throw is central and you can't angle it to your team-mates, where's the advantage to the team taking the line-out?

The advantage comes from the knowledge of where the ball is going to go. A good, well-trained team will practise different tactics and have codewords to alert their colleagues as to the destination of the throw. One of the few things I remember from school rugby, aside from finding stud marks on my throat, was my PE teacher and his belief that he had a secret code that even the Enigma machine would struggle to crack. If the ball was to be thrown to the first player in the row, the hooker would shout 'A'. If it was going to the middle, he would shout 'B'. To the back? That's right, he'd bellow 'C'. Genius. Mind you, it was probably all that our frostbitten brains could cope with.

Proper rugby teams will shuffle in the line, swap places, lift each other up in the air, make decoy jumps, all while shouting out numbers, letters or the names of Buddy Holly records. Befuddle the opposition and someone should be able to jump up and either slap the ball to one of the backs lined up behind their team's row, or take control of it and start a maul.

In this case, your hooker throws the ball up, it is palmed to your backs and your team breaks forwards. Off they go, thundering across the halfway line and you're with them all the way. The ball is passed down the line of backs, you take it and you charge forwards, sidestepping an oncoming defender. As another one approaches you, you pass it sideways to your team-mate on the wing and, leaving two trails of fire on the floor like the Delorean in *Back To The Future*, he accelerates past the opposing full-back and hurls himself over the line, 10 yards in from the right touchline. It's a try and five points to your team. Well done you.

The conversion

As mentioned earlier, every try is followed by a conversion attempt, a kick at goal worth two points. The kick is taken from anywhere in front of the point where the ball was touched down and so, as your team-mate grounded the ball halfway between the posts and the touchline, it's a moderately difficult one for your team.

If your team-mate had been quick enough, not just to get over the line, but to cut in and ground the ball somewhere directly between the posts, the kicker would have a much easier job, but he didn't and so there's no point moaning about it. Especially as this is an entirely hypothetical rugby match, conceived for the purpose of enlightening you about the sport.

The kicker will place the ball on the ground, maybe kicking a divot out of the turf to support its weight, and will then prepare himself. Kicking in rugby has an awful lot to do with nerve, so you'll see most kickers carefully composing themselves before they strike. They'll want to gauge the wind, consider their aim, slow their heartbeat and maybe even assume a slightly fey position, before stepping forwards and doing their thing. If everything goes according to plan and the ball passes between the posts and over the crossbar you'll see the two referee's assistants, or 'touch judges' as they tend to be known, waving their flags in the air. It's a good kick and it's another two points. You're now 7-0 up.

The game will restart with a drop kick from the centre, taken by the team who conceded, and off we go again. There's just enough room for me to tell you about the other way of scoring points, which is to kick a drop goal from open play.

The drop goal

Also known as a 'field goal', a drop goal is like a conversion, but is instead taken from open play. Let's take you back into the flow of our game. Imagine that your team caught the restart kick perfectly and moved forwards looking for another try. As you run past the halfway line, the ball is passed down the line of backs and you progress to your opponent's 22-yard line. They make a good tackle and there is a ruck, which your forwards win. The ball is passed to you, right in the centre of the pitch, 25 yards out. This is the optimum drop kick position. You take the ball in your hands, hold it straight, drop it to the ground and, a split second after it touches the turf, you send it through the posts and above the crossbar with an almighty thump. Three more points! 10-0.

Drop goals are difficult because the opposition will very rarely give you the time to take the ball, take aim and take the points. They'll want to take your kneecaps. There is also a tactical conundrum. If you're close enough to the posts to kick a goal, you're close enough to start a move that could lead to a try. Why take three points when you could get five, and then maybe two more with the conversion? Most players will weigh the potential telling-off that they'll get if they miss, against the increased amount of points on offer for a try, and they'll just pass the ball. Not all teams, though. England won the World Cup in 2003 with a drop goal, scored by Jonny Wilkinson.

Well, there you go. Consider those the bones of your rugby education. Now let's flesh them out by having a look at all the things that can go wrong in a game. The fouls, the infringements, the errors and the penalties. You're well on your way to understanding the game of rugby, but there's a long distance left to travel before you're ready to get roaringly drunk with complete strangers and hold your own in conversation. That's the Holy Grail to which we all aspire, isn't it?

Fouls, infringements and penalties

The knock-on

Right then, let's go back to that kick-off. You know, the one where you got wiped out just after catching the ball? I put an enormous amount of narrative trust in you back there. I assumed that you would be more than capable of catching the ball safely as it came towards you and I stand by that judgement. You were clever enough to buy this book, so I rate you very highly in every department. However, what would have happened if you'd messed it up? I know, I know, it's barely conceivable, but just imagine.

The ball spins through the air and you hold your hands out with your eyes squeezed tightly shut, like a naughty child expecting a slap on the palms with a ruler. The ball hits your hands, bounces up into your chest and then rebounds off in front of you and lands on the ground. Desperate to regain control, you go to pick it up, but the referee has already blown his whistle. You're guilty of a knock-on.

Knock-ons are an extension of one of the first rules you learned. You can't pass the ball forwards with your hands, not even to yourself. They're not exclusive to kick-offs either; they can happen anywhere in the game and have a two-tiered system of punishment. If the referee believes that the knock-on was the result of you and your habit of catching like a six-year-old girl, he'll award a scrum to your opponents. If he believes that you did it deliberately, to gain advantage, he'll award a penalty to the other team, which is much worse, but we'll come to that later.

If you go to catch the ball, fumble it, but regain control of it before it touches the ground, it is not a knock-on. The referee will only blow his whistle if the ball hits the ground or any other player. You'll also be alright if you're one of those death or glory madmen who charge down at players as they go to kick the ball up the pitch, accidentally knocking the ball on in the process, although it has to be said that getting a rugby ball up the snout may cancel out any potential benefits of this manoeuvre, at least on a personal level.

The ruck infringement

Rucks may look chaotic, but there are strict rules governing the way in which they develop. They have to be fair, they cannot be simple 'bundles' and the offside rule is used here to keep some semblance of order.

When a ruck develops, you can only join in to help your team from the back of it. Doing so from anywhere else will result in a penalty to the other team. Imagine that there is a large stone wall running all the way across the pitch with you on one side and the ruck on the other. Directly behind the ruck is a small gateway. This, unless you are Spiderman, is the only means of access to the fray. If you keep this in mind, it is much easier to know where you join in because, with that whopping great wall and one gate, there is only one option. You join from the back.

You will be given offside if you join from the opponent's side because that stops people trying to sabotage the other team's effort to gain control of the ball. Besides, they'd probably give you a good shoeing as soon as you arrived.

You will also be offside if you try to join from anywhere in front of your rearmost team-mate. If a weaker player is first to the ruck then he has to contest it. You can't just squeeze in front of him to add a bit of power to the tussle. You can't come crashing in from the side, and you certainly can't leap on to the top of it.

You can't just hang around and wait to see what happens either. If you're near the ruck, get in it or go away. There is an imaginary line running across the pitch from the back of the hindmost player's hindmost foot and if you're in front of it and not in the ruck, you're offside. It's the same if you leave the ruck, you have to get back behind that offside line.

At the breakdown, the tackler and tacklee are obliged to get out of the way as soon as possible. Now, with lots of other players piling in, that's not always easy, but the referee will take a dim view of any attempts to obstruct the game. If a tackled player attempts to hold the ball either in his hands or by craftily laying on it, a penalty will be awarded. The fallen player can place the ball in an advantageous position, usually towards their oncoming team-mates, but they must do it instantly to avoid punishment.

Those joining the ruck must make sure that they bind with their team-mates, wrapping at least one arm around them as if it were a mini-scrum. It's a team-game, not a free-for-all in a pub car park. They cannot use their hands to pick up the ball;

they can only 'ruck' with their feet to get it behind them and in the direction of their waiting backs. If it all becomes too messy and the ball is deemed unplayable, then the referee will award a scrum to the team moving forwards. If that's not possible, and it really will have had to have been very messy for that, the scrum will be awarded to the team who were moving forwards before the ruck developed.

Offences in open play

Although it may not feel like it if you get hit with a heavy tackle, there are actually some very strict rules governing this part of the game as well. The correct way to tackle a man is to wrap your arms around his legs and squeeze, bringing him to the ground as if you're a human lasso. The next best method is to grab him on the upper body and squeeze, but that really only works if the tackler has a considerable weight or momentum advantage. If a lightweight player grabs a heavy set steam-train of an opponent by the torso, he's more than likely to be worn like a backpack and carried away, and that's just embarrassing.

Anything above the shoulders is dangerous play and will result in a penalty and maybe even a sending-off. A tackle without arms is out as well, you can't just run into people and hope that they fall over. A brief respite is given to any airborne players and no mercy is shown by the referee to anyone who contravenes that law. Hitting a man in the air is likely to cause serious damage. It is also a rather obvious offence, as well as bad manners, to tackle someone who hasn't even got the ball.

The dreaded spear tackle goes way beyond the blurry boundaries of what is and isn't acceptable in rugby. It's the name given to the act of lifting an opponent up into the air and throwing him head or shoulders first on to the ground. If the reprobate or reprobates responsible are fortunate enough to get away without killing or paralysing their victim, they will be unlikely to play rugby for some time afterwards, such is the ferocity of the IRB's stance towards it, although there have been exceptions. In 2003, the British & Irish Lions captain Brian O'Driscoll was injured after being spear-tackled by two members of the New Zealand team, but an independent commissioner decided that the offenders had no case to answer. Needless to say, the Lions begged to differ.

Any form of hitting, slapping, punching, kicking, trampling or tripping will result in a penalty, as will any retaliation to it, although that doesn't mean that you won't see it in almost every rugby match you watch. Rugby is an unashamedly physical affair and a good punch-up comes fitted as standard to most games. They don't whinge, they don't whine, they just hit each other for a while and then get sent off. In a funny kind of way, it's all very honourable.

Obstruction is another regular offence, popular because it's very difficult for the referee to spot. This is quite simply when a player stands in the way of another, preventing him from reaching the ball. Of course, in American football this is actually an established tactic, but there's no room for any of that gridiron nonsense here and it's punishable with a penalty.

Which brings us back to the question of offside once again, which, as you're now probably realising, is a prominent theme in the game of rugby. As I explained earlier, the basic gist of offside is that you can't be in front of the ball-carrier if he is your team-mate. Being in front of an opposition ball-carrier is, of course, perfectly acceptable and championed. It's the best place to tackle him from. Anyway, keep focusing on that simple rule. Get behind the ball-carrier if he's wearing the same shirt as you because if you don't and you become involved in the game, a penalty will be awarded against you.

You can be offside when one of your team-mates wellies the ball forwards from behind you, but there are a number of ways in which you can become onside again. If an opponent gains control of the ball and runs 5 metres, you're back onside. If the opponent runs under 5 metres, but passes the ball, you're back onside as well. If the ball is kicked to the opposition and you are within 10 metres of wherever it lands, you're offside until you retreat the required distance. Simple.

Maul offences

Let's get back to those mauls which, I'm sure you'll remember, are essentially rucks but when all the players are on their feet. For that reason, the same offside rules and entry rules apply. Come in from the back, not the side. Get in it or get out and onside. Bind with your arms to prevent it becoming a free-for-all.

Opposing players cannot be dragged out of a maul, no matter how badly they smell. If they're in there, you have to push even harder or shout for reinforcements. Remember that the key to a maul is to keep things moving. If a maul is stopped in its tracks by a particularly resilient defence, the referee will shout 'use it or lose it' and if it isn't used, he'll award a scrum to the opposing team.

Sometimes in the confusion of a maul two distinct groups will emerge. The ball might be slipped back towards the rear of the maul for protection, but the front of it may push too far forwards, breaking contact. This will lead to something called a 'truck and trailer'. It means that there is one group pushing the opposition and another group, separate to that, carrying the ball. Or, as the referee will see it, one group is obstructing and the other is hiding behind them. A truck and trailer means a penalty against the attacking side.

Scrum offences

The important thing to remember about scrums is that the majority of the rules are in place to stop people breaking their necks. As you'll already have seen, this is a game heavy in machismo and, when you tell a pack of motivated and aggressive men to start pushing, they won't stop pushing just because they feel a bit tired, or feel a bit queasy or feel a bit of vertebra poking through their skin. There have been a number of tragedies in scrums and the game's organisers are very keen not to see any more.

For this reason, binding is pivotal. Referees are very strict on insisting that props, the front row of forwards in a scrum, bind on to the shirts of their opponents and nothing else. This is why, in the introduction, Brian Moore was being naughty by suggesting that you could bind to an opponent's arm in an effort to stop him pushing effectively. The referee will come down hard on anyone who grips on to the collar, face, arm, sleeve, armpit hair or anything else of his opposite number. All other players must bind tightly along their row to create as stable a force as possible. Props must also be careful not to exert downward pressure because that's exactly how spines get broken.

At the first sign of a scrum collapse, the referee will blow his whistle to signal that everyone must stop pushing. Anyone who fails to heed his warning will find themselves in particularly hot water. He will also blow if a player finds himself popping out of the top of the scrum like an over-excited teenager in a limousine, or if anyone is silly enough to be twisting, lowering, pulling, or doing anything that might cause injuries.

Sometimes a scrum will be slightly overbalanced and will start to spin around like a big hairy Catherine wheel. If it goes through more than 90 degrees, the referee will demand a new scrum with the team who didn't have possession getting the put-in. So there's an incentive to behave.

Once all that's sorted and everyone has crouched, touched and engaged, you can get on with the important business of putting the ball in. Mind you, even that is fraught with risk. The ball must be thrown in by the scrum-half, straight down the middle of an imaginary line separating the two packs. You can't angle it, you can't spin it and you can't do the old trick where you mock throwing it in, as if you're pretending to throw a stick for a gullible dog. That really winds people up and the last people you want to upset are forwards.

When the ball gets into the scrum, no one can touch it with their hands except the number eight and the scrum-half. It has to be kicked backwards or kept in possession as the scrum moves forwards.

Author's note:

The ELVs of 2008 also stipulated that the backs should line up 5 yards behind the scrum, in order to create more room for an attack. If they stand too close to the scrum, you see, any territorial advantage is outweighed by the proximity to a large number of big blokes who want to stamp them into the turf. The new law stated that any backs found further forward than 5 yards would be offside. In 2009, the IRB approved the change and passed it into law.

There are some more variants on that offside rule as well. The scrum-half with the put-in has to make sure that he always has one foot behind the ball, so as it travels backwards through his scrum, so does he. His opposite number must obviously have both feet behind the ball as it moves away, otherwise he'll be so far offside that he'll be standing with the opposition backs.

Line-out offences

Line-outs are fairly simple affairs, the key rule being that the ball must be thrown straight down the middle of the two teams. Any shoving, pushing, pulling, slapping or punching is strictly banned, as it's supposed to be a fair contest for possession of the ball.

The offside line here is 10 metres back so if you're not in the line-out, you have to scarper sharpish and wait for the ball to be passed back towards you.

Author's note:

The ELVs of 2008 finally clarified one of the greyer areas of the sport, officially allowing players to lift up their team-mates in the line-out. It didn't make an awful lot of difference to the game as many teams had doing it for years on the sly, but at least they no longer had to be so sneaky about it.

Try 'scoring' offences

One of the saddest sights in rugby, and it happens everywhere from the professional game all the way down to club level, is a try ruled out because the player has lost control of the ball. Sometimes it might not be his fault, but strangely it seems that more often than not, it actually is.

The whole point of a try is to prove to everybody watching that you have the ball and that you have achieved the primary objective of touching it down over the try-line. You can do this two ways. You can treat the act of scoring as seriously as possible and focus on nothing except putting the ball down firmly, or you can fly through the air with a broad grin on your face, showing off to the cameras. The second one is far more memorable, but it's funny how gravity can force a man to suddenly put his arms out in front of him as he approaches the ground...

A try can also be ruled out if the player who puts the ball down allows his feet to cross the touchlines on either side of the pitch. It doesn't matter if the player's entire body is leaning hard over towards the posts, if a single foot has slipped over the line, the ball will be deemed to have gone out of bounds.

On the flip side, it is possible for a try to be awarded to a team without them having to even cross the line. This is a penalty try, awarded when the defensive team has deliberately used nefarious means to prevent a score, like tripping or obstruction. Not only is it an instant five points, but the conversion is awarded from right in front of the posts, so there's likely to be another two points on top of that as well. Unlike their football cousins, rugby players don't resort to fouling when all legitimate methods have failed. It's just not worth it.

Penalties

You will have noticed a number of references to penalties so far in this book with little explanation outside of the implication that they are A Bad Thing. It's time we clarified their status, especially as most people's idea of penalties will have come from football. In that sport, a penalty is a straightforward kick at goal where the goalkeeper has little chance of saving the striker's shot. Penalties in rugby are very different.

For starters, the team's captain will have a choice of how the penalty should manifest itself and there are four main options for him to choose from.

1. A goal kick

The standard choice is to kick at goal as if it were a conversion. A penalty is worth a whopping three points, so if the kick has been awarded anywhere within 40 yards of the posts and is fairly central, you'll usually see the captain go for this option. It's quite possible to win a game on penalties alone and a good kicker can really get those points ticking over. Of course, if he misses then the advantage is lost completely.

2. A scrum

Other captains may prefer to take a scrum. This will give them the put-in and the chance to get an attacking move underway. This is the preferred option of any team with a powerful selection of forwards because they will almost certainly win the scrum and retain possession. They may even simply try to bring the ball under control with their feet in the scrum and then push forwards over the try-line to score five points that way. This is also a good option when facing a team with an organised defence. If you ask for a scrum, you know that all of the opposition's big players will have to contest it, leaving you free to get the ball out to the backs quickly so that they can attack the unprotected zones of the pitch.

3. A 'tap penalty'

If the captain wants to get play underway swiftly, perhaps

because he has seen that the other team have drifted out of position, he can take a 'tap penalty'. By dropping the ball on to his foot and tapping it back into his arms, he can restart the game within moments of the referee's whistle. If his team's backs are particularly quick, he could have the ball out and among them before the other team have finished picking mud out of their ears. It's a high-risk strategy as it means turning down the possibility of kicking for points and, if the team are not disciplined enough, they may not be ready for it.

4. A kick for touch

The final option is to kick for touch. Now you remember how the line-out will always be awarded to the team who didn't touch the ball last? That's not the case if you kick for touch on a penalty. In that instance, possession remains with the team who kicked the ball out of play. This means that a team under heavy pressure in front of their own try-line can win a penalty, welly the ball down the other end of the pitch and then have a line-out close to their opponents' try-line. A significant improvement in their situation, I'm sure you'll agree.

Penalties are also a starting point for looking at the strict control that the match officials have over the players. In rugby, as we'll explore later, the referee has final say and you question his judgement at your peril. When a penalty is awarded, the misbehaving team must immediately retreat 10 yards without even a squeak of protest. Anyone who hangs around to pour scorn over the referee's parentage will cost their team a territorial penalty. The referee can push the penalty 10 yards forwards if he feels that the other team are whining too much. For the attacking team, this could be the difference between a tricky kick and a makeable one, or a makeable one and a sure thing. Hypothetically, a referee can continue to push the penalty forwards in 10-yard increments until the ball crosses the line and a penalty try is awarded. However, the power of the referee is so secure in rugby that very few players would ever be stupid enough to push their luck that far.

Miscellaneous facets of the game

In the interest of making all of that as easy as possible, there were a few concepts that I couldn't include in the framework of our fictional game. In order to make sure that you don't miss a thing, here's a description of some of the other facets of rugby that you may find confusing.

Calling a mark

Catching a swirling rugby ball from a great height is, as we've already discussed, an unenviable task, fraught with personal danger. In order to lessen the amount of casualties on the field, catchers can ease the pressure by shouting their intentions as the ball approaches them. A simple bellow of 'MARK!' will signal that the player wants to clear his lines unmolested, without the possibility of anyone jumping on his head. Assuming that he catches the ball, no one is allowed to tackle him and he will be free to take a kick to get the ball up the other end of the pitch. A mark can only be called within your team's own 22-yard line.

22-metre drop-out

In football, if you kick the ball in your own net you will score an own-goal, a point for the other team. However, in rugby, that's not the case. Under certain circumstances a defender can touch the ball down over his own try-line and then have the chance to essentially kick the match off again from his own 22-yard line. However, it only works if the other team touched the ball last.

You'll usually see it if an attacking team has kicked the ball too far forwards and it rolls over the try-line rather pathetically, miles away from any attacking players who could set it down and score a try. In this instance, a defender can run in and touch the ball down quite safely. He'll then take the ball to his own 22-yard line and restart play with a drop kick.

What he can't do is intercept a pass in front of his own try-line and then scarper back to put it down in the scoring zone. That would result in a 5-metre scrum, which we'll come to in a minute.

The 22-metre drop-out is also used to restart play when the ball goes out over the dead-ball line at either end of the pitch. Kind of like a goal-kick in football, if that helps.

5-metre scrum

If the defending team are silly enough to put the ball down in their own scoring zone and the last touch didn't come from the attacking team, then a 5-metre scrum is awarded. This is the furthest forward that a scrum can be, within sniffing distance of a try, but not so close that one can be scored with a tiny advance of territory. Any scrum awarded for an offence within 5 metres of the line will take place here, preventing any squabbling about positioning the scrum so close to the scoring zone that one good push could seal the deal.

Quick throw

Line-outs don't have to be as regimented as I described. It is quite within a team's rights to take the throw quickly before anyone gets there. However, the player who throws must be the only player to touch the ball. He can't run off the field, pick it up, wait for the best thrower to arrive, pass it to him and then get the game underway. He is also required to use the same ball that was kicked off the pitch, in order to prevent over-zealous ball boys having an influence on the flow of the game. The throw must be taken as normal and thrown a minimum of 5 metres in a straight line. After all of that, it's more than likely that the other players will have arrived and, if the throw hasn't been taken by the time the lines begin to form, the option of a quick throw is lost forever.

Substitutions

The 15 players who start a game are not necessarily the 15 who will end it. A team manager can make changes to his team as the game progresses, or he can have changes forced upon him.

In international matches there are seven spare players on the bench and teams can substitute up to two front-row players and up to five others. They can be used as either outright 'substitutes' or 'replacements'. There is a clear distinction. Let's go back to that game we were discussing. Imagine if you had dropped the kick-off and it was the first of a number of horrible mistakes. You were dropping every pass, you were kicking for touch outside of your own 22-yard line, you were throwing the ball to the opposition. It was genuinely horrible to watch. The manager would have no alternative but to haul you off the pitch and replace you with someone at least halfway competent. This is a substitution.

Now imagine that you were actually doing quite well. You'd scored a try, made some clever moves and even thrown yourself in for a great tackle, but then you pick up an injury, a glancing blow across the head that draws blood. No player can continue to play rugby if he's bleeding, for obvious health reasons. It doesn't necessarily mean that you're out of the game, though. Your manager can make a 'blood replacement', send you to get patched up and then reverse the switch when you are stitched and clean. This is a replacement.

However, there are complications. Let's be honest, it wouldn't be rugby if there weren't. Front-row players, that is to say props and hookers, are treated differently to the rest of the team. Scrums can only be contested if everyone at the front is a specialised front-row forward. It's too dangerous to put a makeweight player in there. Therefore, if one of them is injured, they have to be replaced by one of their own kind, even if he's already been withdrawn. So even if you're a front-row forward who has been substituted for a poor performance, it's not certain that your game is finished. If the new front-row forward is bloodied or injured, you may be the only person who can take over.

If there really are no other options to go at the front, the referee will ask for all scrums to be entirely uncontested with no pushing. The team with the put-in, therefore, will always win possession of the ball.

And that's that! You now know all the basics of the game of rugby union, enough to be able to understand a game as it unfolds in front of you. But what kind of game will you watch and what kind of team will you see? Let's have a closer look at the professional game and how it all works.

The professional game

Referees

You know, I keep referring back to the differences between football and rugby and I must apologise if I sound a little obsessed. I'm just completely fascinated by the way that two games, born out of the same undignified 19th-century melee, have managed to evolve so differently. My favourite contrast is the way in which the match officials are treated by the players.

You don't have to be a football fan to know what goes on when one of their referees makes a controversial decision. The players rise up and snarl at him like animals. They throw their hands up in the air, swearing and shouting, calling him every name under the sun. On the touchline, the managers join in as well. If they can't make their complaints known to the referee, they'll turn on the fourth official. After the game, the reporters will cluster at press conferences, looking for a good headline. 'The referee cheated us, he was appalling! How can he be allowed to officiate?' It's vile and unfair and, outside of hooliganism, it's the most distasteful aspect of the sport.

It would never happen in rugby. Ever.

It doesn't matter how many international caps you've won or how many World Cup-winning drop goals you've scored, every player refers to the referee as 'sir'. They don't argue with him because if they do, he'll start getting angry and no one wants to be around an angry referee. They rule rugby matches like medieval tyrants, sat atop a throne of cruelty, dispensing instant justice or injustice as they see fit. And no one questions them.

There is nothing quite as heartening as the sight of a tiny referee stood in between two misbehaving prop forwards, jabbing his finger at them with barely a thought for his own personal safety. It's like watching a Jack Russell breaking up a fight between two Rottweilers. If he tried to lecture two hulks like that in a city pub the authorities would find his remains in three different alleyways. In this sport, they'll stand completely still and take it all in, meekly apologising and then running away.

In the big games, the referee is miked-up so that you can hear everything he says. This can often provide as much excitement as the match itself. I saw one encounter where a nippy winger seemed to be tripped over by his opponent. The referee thought otherwise.

'Oi!' he bellowed at the offending player in a broad Welsh accent. 'Any more of that and I'll send you to drama school!'

Can you even begin to imagine the fun if the officials were allowed to do that in a football match? I can think of some footballers who'd probably leave the stadium in tears.

Rugby players have to respect referees because the alternative is too risky. At the first sign of dissent, the ball could be pushed forwards 10 yards as a punishment. At the second, the player could find himself sat on the sidelines.

Decades of this kind of authoritarianism have led to an inbuilt subservience as instinctive as a dog's desire to spin round three times before sitting down. With most teams, it's self-policing as well. Argue with a decision and you'll find your own team-mates telling you to zip it.

There is a vague three-tiered system of punishment in rugby, vague because the referee is under no obligation to follow it to the letter. For a first offence, a verbal warning will be handed out. It will be brief, but for the most part humiliating. The miscreant will have his shortcomings highlighted in a very loud voice and he'll have to stand in silence like a naughty schoolboy before apologising and being told to go away. Sometimes, the referee will call the captains together and warn them as well because, in rugby, the captains are responsible for the behaviour of their players. This unofficial 'team caution' means that the next player to offend will be made an example of, even if it's the first offence of his life.

A yellow card can be handed out for a more serious offence, a repeated offence or simply because the referee picked up a parking ticket the other day and he's still really quite peeved by it. It means that the player will be sent to the sidelines, or the 'sin bin' as it is known, for 10 minutes, leaving his team shorthanded and making him the coach's least popular person for a while.

For the really serious stuff, the referee can show a red card and remove the player from the game permanently. This doesn't happen as often as it does in football, for reasons that I'd imagine are fast becoming obvious to you. People just don't take the risk.

But, like the *Yellow Pages*, the referees are not just there for the bad things in life. They can also act as objective coaches to both teams. They won't simply blow the whistle for every offence they see, not if they can have a loud word and clear it up quickly, allowing the game to continue. It must be the only sport in the world where the match officials actually help individuals with their game.

'Green 13,' you'll hear, assuming that a team is playing in green. 'You're offside, step back! Step back, Green 13, that's it, thank you!'

'No hands, Blue 4! No hands!' they'll holler. 'Blue 4? Can you hear ... oh, sod it then.'

PHWEEEP!

'Penalty to Greens, hands in the ruck. Don't look at me like that Blue 4, I warned you!'

For some reason, it works best to read all of that in a Welsh accent. I wish I knew why...

Tactics

With so many different ways to score points and such a wide variety in the shape and size of the players, it's no surprise that a number of different tactics and attitudes have developed across the world. Not every team runs with the ball and not every team tries to score tries. There's more than one way to maul a cat.

Strong

A team blessed with large, powerful players will adapt its game accordingly. There's no point risking a running game if you can push or poke your way through the defensive lines with more chance of success. It's less a case of a hot knife through butter and more a case of a heavy mallet through the front window of a delicatessen.

Scrums will always be chosen when a penalty is awarded because a heavier pack is practically unstoppable if there is a clear weight advantage. If the ball can be retained inside the scrum as it moves forwards, vital yards can be snaffled up in no time so that when the ball is released, it's much, much closer to the goal-line.

A strong team can run riot across the rugby pitch, mauling their way towards the line with impunity. Forwards can make small advantages and welcome the tackle, knowing that that they can stay on their feet. Even rucks are acceptable as, with the big players hitting them first, they are more likely to win those as well.

When a heavier team continually pulverise their opponents there are some very basic, but very clear advantages. The other team become tired and more than a little bit sore, and they will probably become demoralised as well. There's a certain psychological advantage to having an enormous team, especially at close quarters. When you're being repeatedly hit by the bigger boys, it's only natural for your head to drop a little as the game wears on.

Of course, there are more than a few drawbacks with playing rugby like this. The physical game is very predictable. If the only plan is to drive forwards like rampaging trolls, then the opposition always knows what's coming. Without the little sparks of creativity and spontaneity, physical teams can find it difficult to respond quickly to a deficit. It takes a lot longer to maul your way to the try-line than it does to pass your way there.

England played like this in 1991, pushing all the way to the World Cup Final while barely making use of their backs. It was not a tactic that was met with universal approval. Critics described it as a primitive style of play, less exciting on the eye than the rapid and exciting running moves of other teams. The jibes reached their target and England decided to alter their tactics just before the final against Australia. They lost the game 12-6.

Sometimes, it's just best to stick to what you know.

Running

There is nothing quite as beautiful as watching a rugby team who like to run. This is the kind of game that makes the sport so compelling, but part of its magic is in making the so-very-difficult look so-very-easy. A running game, you won't be surprised to hear, works best when the team are blessed with quick backs, packed full of stamina and desire, but that's not all.

It doesn't matter how quick a man is, if there's a very big defender standing in his way, he's not going to make it to the try-line. For the running game to work, it has to be intelligent and it has to be capable of responding to changes in the match.

Watch the movement of the men without the ball in a game and you'll notice that they are not just running in straight lines, trying to probe into the opposition half. They will bob and weave, orbiting each other, feinting and slowing. Some will launch decoy runs with no intention of getting the ball, but just hoping to drag a couple of defenders out of the way for someone else to take advantage of the space.

You're much more likely to see a team who play this type of rugby taking quick tap penalties instead of messing about with scrums. The plan will be to get the ball out quickly, get it to the creative types in the back-line and then find the space to release the super-fast wingers on either flank. Five points for a try are always better than three for a penalty and big scores can be racked up quickly with the right team.

That's not to say that this tactic is without its problems. It is far more difficult to do the simple things when you're always doing them at a sprint. One slip-up at this speed and you could find your team still careering along to the try-line while the opposition gleefully nicks possession away and runs, unopposed, into your half. Mistakes are frequent, but that's what makes it all so exciting.

If you want to see the running game played to perfection, get yourself on to the internet and type 'greatest try of all time' into any search engine. You'll find yourself watching a team called the Barbarians (more on them later) playing New Zealand in 1973. From all the way back on their own try-line, the Barbarians' Phil Bennett somehow manages to evade the attentions of his pursuers, switching direction, ducking and diving and then releasing a team-mate with a perfectly timed pass. The move spreads from their own 22, all the way down the left flank, and is finished off spectacularly by Gareth Edwards who bursts past the last defenders and hurls himself through the air to touch down over the try-line. It'll make you tingle, I assure you.

That's rugby as God intended.

Kicking

If a team is blessed with a player so talented that he could probably kick a rugby ball through a basketball hoop from 60 yards in the middle of a blizzard, then it's more than likely that they're going to build their entire game around him. There are so many points available for kicking and sometimes a team can accumulate them quicker by never even attempting to score a try.

A team focused on the kicking game will usually combine it with the kind of 'phase rugby' we discussed earlier. Most kickers have a preferred foot, so you'll sometimes see the forwards punching holes in a specific side of the defence, and backs actually veering sideways, rather than forwards. The aim of the game here is to hold possession in the side that their kicker favours, thus giving him the best possible chance of stacking up some points.

Naturally, this kind of team will always want to kick their penalties, either at the posts or out to touch to gain a line-out in an advantageous position. Opposing teams will have to be extra careful not to make mistakes, because every offence could cost them three points, leading to a slow and frustrating haemorrhage.

Putting that much responsibility on one single player, however, is just asking for trouble. There are teams out there, sad as it may seem, who will specifically target the kicker and try to injure him. If they succeed, the kicking plan is in tatters. There is also the question of the kicker's own nerve. It only takes a couple of misses or a loss of concentration for the ball to start shanking away from the posts and, if that happens, a rapid rethink is required.

But when this tactic works, goodness me, how it pays dividends. England's World Cup win of 2003 was built on the kicking of Jonny Wilkinson who capped off every team move by calmly slotting the ball between the posts. England set them up, Wilkinson put them away, and there was nothing that even the best rugby-playing nations in the world could do to stop him. In true fairy-tale fashion, he sealed the victory by drop kicking the winning points in extra-time.

Of course, after that he succumbed to a series of injuries that put him on the sidelines for years and, in his absence, England's power in the global game gently ebbed away, but them's the breaks, eh?

Spontaneous

Just as in any sport, an ability to effectively execute multiple styles of play according to conditions and circumstances will always serve a team better than a radical belief in one single doctrine. The best teams in the world are spontaneous, expressive and utterly convinced of their own ability.

The greatest teams will have forwards big enough and brave enough to dominate scrums, win rucks, force mauls and swing the balance of any game. They'll have backs who are as quick as they are clever and they'll have a fly-half and a scrum-half wily enough to quickly analyse an opponent's weak spots and direct the play accordingly. But spontaneity and inspiration come at a price.

The French, for example, are renowned for their ability to switch between defeat-defying daredevilry and hapless incompetence at the twitch of an eyebrow, although that's obviously not the plan at the start of every game. As a nation, they simply tend to play with more freedom than your average international side, always looking to try something impossible and, in the process, usually discovering why no one else shares their reckless nature.

Rugby's best XV

How do you decide upon the greatest rugby team of all time? The task is fraught with difficulties. Can you compare the legends of the amateur game with the highly toned leviathans of today's professional rugby union? Can you single out individuals for special praise in a game that owes so much to the team ethic? Can you hurl them together into an arbitrary fifteen, or XV as they say in these parts? Well, for the purposes of this book, and of passing on just a small chunk of this sport's legacy, yes. Yes, you can.

The following players have been chosen after lengthy debate with every rugby fan I know. Some positions were unanimous; others had a selection of different candidates. In a few years' time, you may come back to this book and completely disagree with every one, although I sincerely hope not. For what it is worth, though, here is rugby union's All-Time Best XV.

Number 15, Full-back – Serge Blanco (France)

If you ever want to offend a French rugby fan, just remind them that Serge Blanco isn't actually French. That should do it. The best full-back ever to grace international rugby was actually born in Venezuela, and was raised in France where he played for Biarritz. Perhaps in an effort to prove his authenticity as a Frenchman, he reportedly smoked 40 cigarettes a day. In spite of this lung-busting habit, he was blessed with extraordinary acceleration, legendary bravery and an admirably cool head under fire.

His finest moment came in the first Rugby World Cup in 1987. With the clock ticking down in their semi-final tie, the French were deadlocked, 24-24, with Australia. Both sides were exhausted and the Wallabies had a line-out just outside the French 22. Somehow, the Europeans managed to snatch possession at a ruck and the ball was Garryowened up the other end of the pitch. France poked and prodded, but couldn't find their way to the try-line until the ball fell to Blanco. With a turn of pace that should have been impossible for a man with 80 minutes of rugby behind him, he burst forwards and surged over the line, sending the French to the first ever World Cup Final. He was a hero to Les Bleus.

Number 14, Right-winger – David Campese (Australia)

Former hairdresser David Campese was arguably the most arrogant rugby player ever to walk the earth. As a Test debutant, he was asked if he was nervous to be marking All Black legend Stu Wilson. 'Stu who?' he replied. And that's just a taster. He boasted of being the first rugby millionaire, despite the fact the game was still ostensibly amateur, repeatedly tried to catch the ball with one hand in important games and mouthed off to anybody who would listen.

Annoyingly, though, he was also one of the most talented players of all time. His trademark goose-step bamboozled his opponents for years and he matched his fearsome pace with an impetuous desire to push the boundaries of the game. Hence all that one-handed nonsense. Still, give him his dues. After gleefully writing England off in the 2003 World Cup, he swallowed his pride and walked up and down Oxford Street in London wearing a sandwich board with 'I Was Wrong!' written on it. So he's not all bad.

Number 13, Outside centre – Brian O'Driscoll (Ireland)

There are not many players better at putting points on the board than Brian O'Driscoll. The Dublin-born centre is Ireland's all-time top try-scorer and he's banging on the door of the international all-time top ten. One of the world's best ever centres, his handling is near-perfect and he has a surge of power that can take him through the smallest of gaps in a defence. O'Driscoll is a living legend for Irish rugby fans, the spearhead of their nation's revival on the international scene. He's also a stalwart of the British & Irish Lions, having been picked in three consecutive tours, starting in 2001.

Mind you, his career and maybe more could have been ended in New Zealand in 2005 when Tana Umaga and Keven Mealumu spear-tackled him in the opening exchanges of a bad-tempered Test match. O'Driscoll, who was captaining the British & Irish Lions at the time, was lifted into the air and hurled head first at the ground. He only just managed to thrust out an arm to protect himself, dislocating his shoulder on impact. Thankfully he made a full recovery and, in the spring of 2009, he led the Irish to their first Grand Slam since 1948.

Number 12, Inside centre – Philippe Sella (France)

France dominated the Five Nations during the 1980s and while Serge Blanco was a vital component of the Gallic machine, Philippe Sella was every bit as important to Les Bleus. The quick-handed centre racked up 111 appearances for his nation over a long career that began in 1982 at amateur Agen in France and ended in 1999, as a professional at Saracens. Sella was a devastating player, mainly because of a combination of skills, nicely summed up by one of his coaches who claimed that he had 'the strength of a bull but the touch of a piano player.'

He could also pass superbly and he had the pace to run, the intelligence to find the gaps and a quite prodigious rate of try-scoring. In 1986 he achieved the rare feat of scoring a try in every Five Nations fixture that season, something that had only ever been achieved by three other players, and only by one man since. All in all, you couldn't ask for a safer pair of hands in your midfield.

Number 11, Left-winger – Jonah Lomu (New Zealand)

There wasn't very much you could do about Jonah Lomu. Having him on the pitch never seemed entirely fair. He was quicker than everyone, bigger than everyone, and harder than everyone. In a game still struggling with the transition from amateur to professional, he became its first genuinely global superstar: part figurehead, part circus freak. At almost 6 and a half feet and nearly 20 stone, tackling him was like trying to tackle the 9.15 from Paddington. You could try, but it would almost certainly leave you smeared across the landscape as a warning to others.

'He's a freak, the sooner he goes away, the better,' scowled mean-spirited England captain Will Carling when he appeared on the scene, but who could blame him? Lomu obliterated his back-line in the 1995 World Cup and would do the same in 1999. He was even headhunted by the National Football League (NFL – the largest professional American football league in the world), although nothing came of it. Thanks to New Zealand's curiously poor record on the main stage, Lomu never won a World Cup, but he certainly won't be forgotten in a hurry.

Number 10, Fly-half – Jonny Wilkinson (England)

Quite simply, the finest kicker of a rugby ball in the game's history. Composed under pressure and relentlessly successful, Surrey-born Wilkinson has scored more World Cup points than any other player, most of them with his natural left foot. The most important score, though, his 2003 World Cup-winning drop goal, was with his right. A bit of a perfectionist, Wilkinson didn't like only being able to kick from one side of the pitch, so he trained himself to be more ambidextrous. How fortunate for England that he did.

Sadly, it was almost four years before he played for them again. Cursed with injuries, he was forced to watch from the sidelines as the national side declined in his absence. He was able to return in time for the 2007 World Cup, but on this occasion England were defeated in the final by South Africa. It should also be noted that, far from being a one-trick pony, he was actually an accomplished fly-half, excelling in both attack and defence for England. He also seemed like a jolly nice chap as well, if that helps.

Number 9, Scrum-half –
Gareth Edwards (Wales)

Scorer of the greatest try of all time, voted the greatest player of all time and, along with David Lloyd George and Tom Jones, probably the greatest Welshman of all time, Gareth Edwards is the definitive scrum-half. The figurehead of the great Welsh rugby sides of the 1970s, he was so talented that he could have succeeded at any sport. Signed by Swansea City Football Club at 16 and capable of competing in the long jump at international level, the boy was a prodigy.

As a player he was incomparable. The quick hands, the cunning, the blistering turn of pace that helped him survive against the tough tacklers; Edwards was the spark plug of the side, igniting sweeping move after sweeping move. As a man, he is a legend, attributing his success to the quality of his team-mates and never allowing his feet to leave the ground.

'I was part of a country that had rugby in its veins,' he said once. 'For a short time I was part of its national side which stretched out for the top and reached a pinnacle. I am thankful for that.'

There wasn't really any other choice for this position.

Number 8, Number eight –
Zinzan Brooke (New Zealand)

The number eight position is one that requires great versatility and there were few players as multi-talented as Zinzan Brooke. A big forward with the cutting pace and power of a back, he played 58 tests for the All Blacks during the 1990s and over 100 in total. For his club side, Auckland, he also played in several other positions including hooker and lock forward, but it was at number eight where he made his name. It wasn't just his combination of strength and speed, it was also his ability to size up situations quickly and his bravery in reaching a swift decision that may not always have been the easiest.

Typifying his career was the moment of the 1995 World Cup during the Lomu-inspired demolition of England when he scored an audacious drop goal from just past the halfway line, over 40 yards away from the posts. You don't get many forwards who can do that, but that mighty kick was no one-off. He did it again, the following year, against South Africa.

Number 7, Openside flanker – François Pienaar (South Africa)

A South African legend immortalised by the 1995 World Cup win, François Pienaar is one of the sport's genuine heroes. With South Africa making the difficult transition from the apartheid regime, Pienaar went to great lengths to make sure that the team he captained was representative of the entire nation, and not just the white bits. With only one black player in the squad this was no easy task, but he stuck to it with the same determination that he brought to his game.

A powerful flanker and an inspirational leader, Pienaar lifted his team in the face of great media scrutiny. The Springboks, having been out of international rugby for years, were ranked only ninth in the world in 1995, but, with wins over Western Samoa, France and Australia, he dragged them to the final where they beat New Zealand in extra time, with Pienaar playing through the pain of a calf injury. His friendship with Nelson Mandela continued long after the World Cup win, so much so that the former president is godfather to one of Pienaar's children. You can read more about that amazing game in the World Cup section on page 81.

Number 6, Blindside flanker – Richard Hill (England)

Known as 'the silent assassin', Richard Hill was a ferocious weapon in Sir Clive Woodward's England arsenal. Despite a fine line in long passes, Hill was often noticed more on the occasions when he wasn't there, specifically in the Lions tour of 2001 when his injury was the turning point of the series. Hence the nickname, you see. Other players made the headlines, but the real damage was done by Hill.

His greatest strength was that he never knew how to give up. He would be the first to every breakdown, the first to stick his face into the danger zone and he often posed such a risk at any ruck that his opponents had to deploy more men to contend with him, which then left more space for his team-mates to exploit. A mild-mannered man off the pitch, he was a lion when he stepped onto it. A key figure in the 2003 World Cup-winning side, the opposing coach Eddie Jones described him as the glue that held England together and as the one player he would want in his own team. A series of injuries and operations has meant that Hill now walks with a permanent limp, a constant reminder of the lengths he went to in order to secure victory for his team.

Number 5, Lock – Martin Johnson (England)

One of the most inspirational figures in the history of English rugby, Martin Johnson was less a man and more a force of nature. You just wouldn't argue with a chap of his size (6 foot 8 inches and over 18 stone), which explains why in 2003, when he told his weakened six-man England scrum to 'get down and shove,' against an eight-man All Black pack, they did so without asking any questions like 'How?', 'Why?' or 'Can I go home now?' When asked afterwards what went through his mind at that moment, he disarmingly replied, 'My spine.'

Johnson led England to the World Cup that year, but was at the helm of the team for many more successes than that. An astonishingly driven man, he was prone to the occasional act of gamesmanship, like leading his team to the wrong bit of the pre-match red carpet at Lansdowne Road against Ireland and refusing to leave, forcing the Irish president to walk on the grass. A succession of stewards thought about asking him to move, but in the end everyone just felt safer leaving him be, and you can hardly blame them. In a physical sense, he took as much as he gave, which is why his face looks like it's been hammered out of a sheet of silly putty. Don't tell him I said that, though. Please.

Number 4, Lock – Frik Du Preez (South Africa)

A legend of 1960s rugby, Frik Du Preez was voted South Africa's Player of the Century in 2000, quite an achievement given what the contemporary squad had managed to do just five years earlier. Du Preez, unusually for a lock forward, was a real all-rounder. Like most forwards, he was utterly fearless and apparently impervious to pain, but he combined his physical strength with an unlikely turn of pace that allowed him to burst through the opposing lines and he could even kick accurately as well.

But it was his off-the-field behaviour that marked him out as something special. Polite and warm, he is often pointed to as an example of how superstars should behave. He showed humility and grace and was a much-loved figure in the game.

Dr Danie Craven, one of the greatest figures in South African rugby, once paid tribute to Du Preez's career. 'As long as rugby is played in our country,' he said, 'people who know Frik or knew him, or people who have heard of him or read about him, will have a connection with him and that will enrich our rugby, just as Frik did on our playing fields.'

Number 3, Tighthead prop – Carl Hayman (New Zealand)

Many rugby fans would make a good case for Carl Hayman being the finest tighthead prop of all time. Signed by Newcastle in 2007 on reportedly the biggest contract ever awarded to a rugby player, his presence gives any front row strength and composure. Not so much strength and composure that Newcastle would ever threaten to win the league, but let's not expect miracles. He's only one man.

It is Hayman's technique in the scrum that has made him so sought after. He isn't any bigger, stronger or faster than any other prop forward who has ever played, but he rarely has to take a step backwards when the pushing starts. He is single-minded, resolute and practically impossible to overpower. Outside of rugby, he can't stand being anywhere near the city and his love of the great outdoors is so well known that the New Zealand rugby authorities attempted to buy him a farm to convince him to stay on the islands.

Number 2, Hooker – Sean Fitzpatrick (New Zealand)

An inspirational leader of men, Sean Fitzpatrick played for the All Blacks from 1986 to 1997, winning almost 100 caps in the process. Possessing excellent handling skills and impressive mobility, and able to deliver a line-out so accurately that you'd swear it was laser-guided, there are few hookers who could compare to him. His reading of the game was also excellent, allowing him to be in the right place at the right time to finish off moves, and he ended his career with 55 points on the board.

Not only is he one of the few New Zealand greats to have ever actually won a World Cup, but he was able to lead the All Blacks to famous victories throughout his career. He took them to a series win over the British & Irish Lions in 1993, before bettering that in South Africa when he became the first New Zealander to captain his side to a Test win there. A clean sweep in the first ever Tri Nations isn't a bad little feather in his cap either. Now a greatly respected expert of the game, you wouldn't rule out seeing him in a coaching role before long.

Number 1, Loosehead prop – Os Du Randt (South Africa)

South African prop Os du Randt was a monster of a man. Weighing in at very nearly 20 stone, he was the absolute last thing that any forward would want to see as the pack closed down around him. At one point the most capped Springbok of all time, a record now surpassed, he is a cult hero in South African rugby and arguably the finest in his position of all time. His real name is actually Jacobus, but 'Os' is Afrikaans for 'ox' and, given the size and strength of the man, it seems more appropriate somehow.

Du Randt's South African career was divided into two chunks. He was a proud member of the 1995 World Cup-winning side, but a series of injuries meant that he spent three years out of the game. Convinced that he would never play rugby again, he became depressed and overweight, even for him. Fortunately, he was eventually persuaded to play club rugby again and he soon caught the attention of the South African coach. Against all the odds, he returned to the Springboks, cemented his place in the team and ended up playing for the 2007 World Cup-winning side as well. Comeback complete, he retired immediately after the final.

The competitions

International
The Rugby World Cup

The premier competition in rugby union is, of course, the World Cup. Organised by the IRB and contested every four years, it is the ultimate test for a professional rugby player and it has been the source of many of the greatest moments in the sport's recent history. Rugby's traditional fear of professionalism meant that the first World Cup didn't take place until 1987, but since then it has grown in strength and now commands huge global television audiences.

Twenty nations gather to play for the Webb Ellis Cup, named rather tweely after that man who probably didn't do that thing that he's famous for, and they are separated into four pools of five teams. These pools are seeded, firstly to ensure that there is a good spread of quality throughout the competition and secondly to make sure that none of the big nations gets wiped out before the lucrative later stages.

All the teams in a group play each other once, and the first stage of the competition rumbles on until a final league table is drawn up, with points for winning counting first, and bonus points for margins of victory used to separate tied teams. The top two teams in each group progress to the knockout stage.

By now, there are just eight teams remaining. Traditionally this would be the big teams from the Southern Hemisphere (Australia, New Zealand and South Africa) and the big five from the Northern Hemisphere (England, Scotland, Wales, Ireland and France). However, as rugby continues to grow in popularity, other nations have begun to flex their muscles.

Fiji, Argentina, Italy and Tonga have all caused the old powers problems in recent years, and nations like Romania, Japan and Canada are quite capable of picking off the establishment if the latter decide to take a game for granted.

Knockout stage games are played, like all rugby matches, for 80 minutes. If the score is tied at the end, a 20-minute period of extra time is played. If there is still no leader at the end of that, the next point, however it comes, wins the tie. The knockout stages sort the teams from eight, to four, to a final pairing of two, which is of course the Rugby World Cup Final.

The most memorable World Cup Final for any Englishman would always be 2003 when Jonny Wilkinson kicked that extra-time drop goal to beat Australia in their own backyard, a result that acted as a catalyst for a truly fearsome day of drinking, given that the celebrations in the UK began at about 9.30am.

Other, more objective observers would claim that the greatest final came in 1995 when South Africa lifted the trophy. What was so special about that? Well, South Africa had been excluded from all sports for decades due to their government's belief that white people had to be separated from black people because, well, they never really came up with a good reason. When Nelson Mandela's ANC party won the first free elections and brought some democracy back to the country, the sports teams were allowed to compete again. South Africa hosted the World Cup, somehow managed to win it, and the trophy was handed to white captain François Pienaar by black President Mandela in one of the most universally appreciated moments of sporting history.

Of course, there are still those people who believe that the funniest moment of Rugby World Cup history was the sight of England being comprehensively dismantled by a Jonah Lomu-inspired New Zealand in 1995. You remember how I said that wingers tended to be quick, lithe chaps? Well, Lomu, as you'll have seen above in the greatest XV, was 6 foot 5 inches and 18 stone and he could outrun a train if he put his mind to it. Scottish, Welsh and Irish fans were united in their mirth when he stormed through England's defence on four occasions in their World Cup clash, at one point going through Tony Underwood simply by ignoring him. Underwood would have had more luck tackling a bear.

The Six Nations

The highlight of any rugby fan's year is the Six Nations, an annual tournament contested by England, France, Italy, Wales, Scotland and Ireland. It's like a mini-season, squeezed into the weeks leading up to Easter, and it can be utterly compelling. Italy are a relatively new addition to the roster, having made their bow in 2000 after a series of impressive World Cup performances. Prior to their arrival, it was just the Five Nations.

The competition couldn't be simpler. All the teams play each other once, with the venues shifting between home and away every year. Two points are awarded for a win, one for a tie and none for a defeat. At the end of the season, the team with the most points wins the championship. It works so well that you wonder why other competitions insist on having pools, play-offs and bonus points.

If two teams have identical points totals, the winner is the team with greatest difference between the match points they have scored and the match points they have conceded. If there's a tie there as well, it comes down to the team who scored the most tries and if they still can't be separated then the organisers give up and tell them to share the trophy.

It is the competitions within the competition that can make the Six Nations so fascinating. The ultimate goal is to win a Grand Slam, which is to defeat every opponent in the course of the competition, securing maximum points in the process. This isn't actually as rare you might think, the gathering momentum tending to inspire a repeatedly victorious team against their rivals.

The home nations (England, Scotland, Wales and Ireland) have their own mini-Grand Slam for beating every other home nation, called the Triple Crown. For decades, this was a mythical prize. Teams would boast of winning 'it', but there wasn't actually an 'it' to win. It was only in 2006 that the sponsors actually made a trophy to commemorate the achievement. The ferocity of rivalry between the home nations is so intense that, should a Grand Slam chance be lost against France or Italy, the Triple Crown, and the local bragging rights that come with it, are usually a decent compensation package.

England's clash with Scotland is always known as the Calcutta Cup thanks to one of those fantastically long-winded and improbable stories that only the British Empire could ever generate. Rugby, you see, didn't take as well in 19th-century India as it did in other far-flung regions of the dominion and the Calcutta Football Club, these being the days when rugby teams still thought of themselves as football teams, had a tough time recruiting members. For one thing, it was too hot to go running up and down for 80 minutes and, for another, the rock solid ground didn't exactly make repeatedly hitting the deck an appealing prospect for your average British gentleman. The club withered and eventually the founding members decided to disband. But rather than taking the club money and splitting it up, or putting it in a whip for a good, honest drinking binge, they decided to do something a little more permanent. The silver rupees from the club safe were melted down and sculpted into a trophy which was presented to the RFU in 1878, the only condition being that they had to award the trophy on an annual basis. The RFU, not wanting to look a gift horse in the mouth, designated it as the trophy for the England–Scotland games, and when the Home Nations Championship, the forerunner of the Five Nations, grew around it, the Calcutta Cup was kept on as a competition within a competition.

There are others too. France and Italy now play for the Giuseppe Garibaldi Trophy, in memory of the Nice-born Italian revolutionary. The Centenary Quaich, which sounds like something Harry Potter might compete for, is actually the Gaelic-themed Ireland and Scotland trophy and the Millennium Trophy is awarded for the winners of England's clash with Ireland.

Superiority in the Six Nations tends to be wave-like. Teams rise up with golden generations and then slip away into the shadows when the key players age and can't be replaced. The French were the dominant force of the 1980s and any Welshman worth his salt will be able to tell you about their great sides in the 1970s. The beauty of the competition is that every game carries some cultural weight, a chance to get one over your neighbours or to correct an old injustice.

As with all rugby matches, the atmosphere is magnificent. There is little of the hatred or casual racism that still blights football. You won't hear sectarian or nationalistic chanting at Twickenham (the largest rugby union stadium in the UK) when Ireland come to visit, nor will you shudder with trepidation if you jump off the train and bump into the opposition's support. The Six Nations is about dressing up and drinking, singing a lot and maybe falling over. Isn't that the way that all sport should be?

The Tri Nations

The Tri Nations is essentially the equivalent of the Six Nations, but for the big Southern Hemisphere teams: New Zealand, Australia and South Africa. Conceived in 1996 immediately after the advent of professionalism, the competition was originally designed on a simple home and away basis, with each nation playing four games. This was extended to include three fixtures against each team in 2006 and 2008, although it reverted back to type for one year only, the World Cup year of 2007.

The competition is a little more complicated than the Six Nations. For starters, there are four points for a win and two for a draw. There are also bonus points, included to promote attacking rugby. Any team that scores four tries or more automatically picks up one bonus point and if the losing team finish seven match points or fewer behind their opponents, they score an extra bonus point for their endeavour. Therefore, the victors will score four or five points, and the losers can score up to two points.

The Tri Nations attracts enormous crowds, sometimes up to six figures, as well as millions of TV viewers. Despite their relative lack of success in the World Cup, an inexplicable trend in itself, New Zealand have dominated the Tri Nations, winning more times than any other nation by some distance. There is something quite glorious about the sight of the All Blacks in full flow. Very physical, but innately gifted, they have a special aura about them in international rugby.

There has been talk of inviting a fourth nation, Argentina, to join in the fun, an idea that has widespread support throughout the world's rugby unions. Their involvement will be dependent on the acquiescence of the major TV companies who control the way the tournament is played, but the general feeling is that it is only a question of when, so watch this space. Or, if it's already happened by the time you read this book, watch *that* space and congratulate me on my prescience.

The European Cup

With professionalism opening the doors to a tide of money, it was only natural that rugby would take its lead from football. Once the concept of competition was officially acceptable, what could be better than competing against everyone in your country to earn a crack at a competition with everyone in Europe? Like football's UEFA Champions League, the European Cup has become the glamour trophy of the club game, the place where everyone aspires to be.

Of course, it hasn't always been so glamorous. It is still rugby after all, and it always takes a few years of arrogant posturing from the unions before they can ever agree on something sensible. The early years of the competition took place without the involvement of English and Scottish clubs, in unbalanced pools including weaker Romanian sides that were little more than cannon fodder for the mighty French clubs. England joined in for the second season, 1996, but then dropped out again in a huff in 1998, only to return in 1999.

Gradually, the competition began to evolve and wrap itself around each nation's domestic calendar, but that hasn't quite stopped the disputes. There were further wranglings between England and France in 2007 as the tournament threatened to eclipse preparations for that year's World Cup.

Assuming everything is sorted out off the field, 24 teams enter the European Cup; their qualification is dependent on their performance in their own domestic league and is limited to the clubs of the Six Nations. Romania were included in the first competition but have since been consigned to the secondary competition, the Challenge Cup. Each nation sends their best teams, according to a reasonably straightforward and meritocratic system.

The top six from France and England join the top three from Ireland and Wales, the top two from Scotland and the top two from Italy. The sharper-minded reader will have noted that the Celtic League has eight representatives from its ten members, a huge portion of potential glory which makes it all the more embarrassing for the two who miss out.

There is a play-off match to decide one of the two remaining places, fought between the ninth-placed team in the Celtic League and the third-placed Italian team. The final place is awarded to the nation who has provided the most recently successful team. So, for example, if Leicester win the Cup, the next year will see seven English teams in the fray.

The lucky 24 teams are divided into six pools of four where they play each other home and away. The pools are decided by a very complicated seeding system which I'm not even halfway clever enough to explain here. Suffice to say that every team's progress in previous competitions is taken into account to generate a giant points-based league table, ordering clubs by their success. The previous winner and the five most historically successful teams are first seeds and the rest are grouped off and drawn to ensure that all pools have a good cross-section of talent and, obviously, to make sure that all the marketable, popular teams don't end up in the same group.

The usual rules apply with the group stages. Four points for a win, two for a draw and those omnipresent bonus points are back again, one for four tries or more and one for losing by seven points or fewer. You're getting the hang of this now, aren't you?

Once all the group games are complete, the six winners progress to the quarter-finals and are joined by the two best-performing second-placed teams. They are then all ordered again according to the amount of points they've scored. The top four win the right to play at home against a randomly drawn second-seeded club.

The semi-finals are played at neutral venues, but in the home country of the first team to be picked out of the hat. In the past this has meant teams like Leicester playing at Leicester City's football stadium, or Irish side Munster playing at Lansdowne Road (a stadium once owned by the Irish Rugby Football Union). It's a neutral venue but, you know, only just.

The final is held at a pre-arranged venue, usually at one of the Six Nations' national stadiums, but not necessarily in the country of either of the finalists. This usually means an enormous booze-cruise as tens of thousands of rugby fans descend upon a random European city and drink its pubs dry.

The Challenge Cup

It's easy to dismiss the Challenge Cup as a spare part, a consolation prize for the teams who fail to reach the more prestigious European Cup, but it's really far more than that. It's an opportunity for the best teams from rugby's secondary nations to gain experience at a higher level. The sport isn't just limited to the Six Nations. Rugby union has long been popular in Romania and is growing in Spain, Germany and even Russia. If it is to have any hope of setting down roots in these countries, there needs to be a chance for them to test their skills against the best. Or, at least, the second best in any case.

The format is very similar to the European Cup, although the numbers are liable to change depending on the interest and ability of the lesser nations. Five pools of four are drawn and the winners of each group join the three best runners-up in the quarter-finals. The semi-finals, played at the home stadium of the first team out of the hat, generate the two finalists, who battle it out for the cup at a neutral venue.

Domestic
The English Premiership

Domestic rugby took a long time to organise itself in the UK. The persistent feeling that leagues would lead to competition, which in turn would lead to poor people having more time to practise and get really good, was reason enough for the RFU to try to prevent their development. In 1987, they finally yielded and allowed the formation of the Courage Leagues, under the banner of the brewing giant. After decades of teams organising their own fixtures and tours with no clearly defined aims, these new leagues were a phenomenal success.

When the sport turned professional in 1995, the big sponsors came in and started to shake things up. A lucrative and high-earning league became a 'Premiership' in 2000, but the organisers tripped over themselves trying to contrive excitement and messed it up. Where there had once been a simple league of teams playing each other home and away to decide the champions, they tagged a play-off on to the end of it. Now the winners of that were the real winners. Or were they? Even the organisers were not sure. At one point, two prizes were handed out, one for the winners of the league, another for the winners of the play-off. Finally, in 2002, they got their act together.

Now the league comprises 12 teams playing each other home and away. At the end of the 22-round season, the top four move into the play-offs. The league leaders are rewarded for their consistency with a home semi-final against the team in fourth, while the third-placed club travel to the home of the runners-up. The two winning sides then meet in a winner-takes-all, make-or-break grand final at Twickenham.

Like the Tri Nations, the points have been tweaked to try to promote excitement. There is a single-point bonus for a team that scores four tries or more, and another for a team that loses by seven points or fewer so that, again, teams can score anything from nought to five points per game. Aside from that, it's the usual two points for a draw and four points for a win. At the end of the season, the bottom-placed team are relegated from the Premiership to the National League, assuming that the champions of that secondary division have a club, a stadium and facilities that meet the minimum standards criteria.

The league still suffers a little from having to compete directly against football at the weekends, but there have been moves to combat this disadvantage. Many games are televised and screened at 3pm on a Saturday, when live domestic football can't be screened in the UK. Other matches are played on Friday nights, to sidestep the lure of football altogether. Harlequins play the occasional game at Twickenham and promote tickets extensively. Year after year, the attendances and press coverage improve and, now that the format has finally been set in stone, domestic rugby can only go on to grow in strength and popularity.

The National League
Beneath the English Premiership lurks an enormous pyramid of mainly semi-professional or amateur club rugby. The Championship, or the second division, contains a number of former Premiership teams, competing against the up-and-coming sides from around the country. Relegation from the Championship leads to National League One, which is split into two regional leagues from the north and the south.

Promotion and relegation operates between the leagues, but because of the financial problems and relatively embryonic state of professional club rugby, it isn't always straightforward.

The Celtic League
While the other rugby unions around the world were falling all over themselves to take full advantage of professionalism, Scotland, Ireland and Wales were strangely reticent. They kept faith in their domestic leagues, realising only in 2001 that there was so much to be made of this brave new world. Having waited too long to join up with other federations, they formed their own Celtic League.

Like their counterparts in England, their early attempts at competition were muddled and ill-thought out. The Celtic League lurched from a simple round-robin to a cup competition, to an unholy hybrid of the two before settling down into just a simple league. The long-awaited stability and the formation of new regional teams helped to attract big-name sponsorship and the all-important attention of the TV companies.

The Celtic League is now ten teams, playing each other home and away across the 18-round season. Like the English Premiership, there are four points for a win, two for a draw and those two bonus points, one for scoring four tries or more and another for losing by seven points or fewer.

The Anglo–Welsh Cup

There is no longer any single club cup competition in rugby, but there are two tournaments to fill the void. The first, and most important, is the Anglo–Welsh Cup, contested by all 12 English Premiership sides and the four Welsh regional clubs. Given rugby's apparent addiction to group stages, it's no surprise that the tournament begins with four pools of four, playing each other once, with the top two qualifying for the knockout stage. The groups are picked specifically according to geography, with teams always playing local rivals, reversing the home and away status every year. It's a good way of boosting attendances, with fans always eager to get one over 'that lot down the road'.

You might wonder why only the Welsh are involved and you'd be right to. Their decision to join in almost saw them kicked out of the Celtic League. The Scottish and Irish teams, probably a little offended that *they* hadn't been asked to play, were even more angry when they discovered that there might be a clash of fixtures. Thankfully, common sense won out and the Welsh were readmitted to the league, and allowed to compete in the cup competition.

The British and Irish Cup

The British and Irish Cup is a secondary competition for the smaller and the semi-professional teams in the Northern Hemisphere. 24 sides are invited from England, Scotland, Ireland and Wales, a healthy mix of reserve teams and second flight clubs.

The teams are divided into four pools of six, playing each other once during international weeks when everyone else is watching the Autumn internationals or the Six Nations. The top team in every pool qualifies for the semi-finals and then a final is held in May.

The absence of the big boys means that it's a shot at glory for some of the smaller, less fashionable teams like the Cornish Pirates or those wonderfully named Rotherham Titans.

9 Teams you should know about

England

It will be a long time before any Englishman forgets the World Cup win of 2003 and the 20-17 extra-time victory over Australia. The English were the first European side to win a tournament that had been dominated by the Southern Hemisphere and they did it in some style, with a Jonny Wilkinson drop goal right at the end of the final. Prior to that, the nearest they had been was to lose the final in their own backyard in 1991.

England have won more Grand Slams than any of their rivals, although the dominance of the early 1990s has now passed them by. They play their home games at Twickenham on the outskirts of London, where three tiers of fans serenade them with the unofficial rugby anthem 'Swing Low, Sweet Chariot'.

Scotland

Scotland's greatest moment came in 1990 when England arrived at the Scots' Murrayfield home for a winner-takes-all clash that would decide the destiny of the Calcutta Cup, the

Triple Crown, the Five Nations championship and, as neither side had lost a game, the Grand Slam as well. England were the runaway favourites, but the Scots simply ignored the odds. Fuelled by rumours that celebratory tee-shirts had already been printed south of the border, they refused to yield and ran out 13-7 winners.

Since then, the glory days have been few and far between. England took their revenge a year later in the semi-finals of the World Cup and Scotland haven't been able to breach the quarter-finals since. A solitary Five Nations championship win is all they have been able to muster since that glorious day in 1990.

Ireland

There are no borders in Irish rugby – the national team represents both the southern and northern sections of the country. That in itself is an astonishing success given the sectarianism that blights other sports in the region. The Irish are a spirited side, but went 61 years without a Grand Slam, finally landing a clean sweep in 2009 to go with their lonely 1948 victory. Players like Keith Wood and Willie John McBride may have missed out on that glory, but they always showed the spirit and determination that their fanatical supporters desired.

Wales

There are few nations on this earth as passionate about rugby as the Welsh and watching one of their games is an experience in itself. The crowd are colourful and loud and the players respond on the pitch with whole-hearted performances. Wales enjoyed their best period in the 1970s when an outstanding group of players all peaked at the same time. Gareth Edwards,

Barry John and JPR Williams were just three of the names to gain immortality after a series of Grand Slams and heroic touring victories.

Although the 1980s and 1990s were a significant departure from those glory days, the 21st century has seen a return to prominence for the Welsh. Grand Slams in 2005 and 2008 were richly deserved and they were only a penalty kick away from securing another in 2009.

France

The French, known as 'Les Bleus', are one of the most exciting international rugby sides on the planet, simply because you can never be sure what they're going to do next. Capable of playing the strongest nations off the park one day and dissolving in front of the weakest on the next, you just never know what you're going to get with them.

France have been playing in the Five/Six Nations since 1910, but they were actually expelled between 1932 and 1947 after allegations of professionalism. Their most successful period came in the 1980s when they won two Grand Slams, but they have never quite managed to go all the way and win the World Cup. Runners-up in both 1987 and 1999, global domination continues to elude them.

New Zealand

Despite having failed to win a World Cup since the inaugural 1987 tournament, New Zealand are still one of the most feared teams on the planet. Clad in all black, hence their nickname, they are ferocious, intimidating and very, very difficult to beat. They've dominated the Tri Nations since its inception in 1996.

The All Blacks prepare for every game with an aggressive war dance in the centre of the pitch, traditionally the Ka Mate variant of the Haka, although occasionally it can be the Kapo o Pango. Ka Mate has been used since 1906 and involves an awful lot of thigh-slapping and shouting, and contains lines like 'Tenei te tangata puhuruhuru nana i tiki mai whakawiti te ra,' which roughly translates as 'This is the hairy man who has caused the sun to shine again for me.' Make of that what you will.

The Kapo o Pango, in use since 2005, is even more terrifying, completed as it sometimes is with a thumb drawn slowly across the throat. That one got a few complaints when it was first used.

The Haka, as all variants are invariably known, is a genuinely astonishing sight. But then fifteen men jumping up and down, screaming and slapping themselves generally is. The reaction of the opposition, however, can often be even more entertaining. While most teams line up a respectful distance back, some foolish souls walk right up to the All Blacks and stare in their faces. In 2008, the entire Welsh team stood in a straight, unblinking line for the whole dance and refused to move at the end of it, staring their tormenters down. The New Zealanders glared back at them imperiously. For a full minute, the referee tried to get the game started, but no one wanted to back down. There isn't a pyrotechnic display in existence that could have roused the crowd to greater heights. Finally, the All Blacks moved away and the game could begin. The Welsh had made their point, but the New Zealanders made theirs in the 80 minutes that followed. They won 29-9.

Australia

Australia were the first nation to win a second World Cup, with their 1999 triumph complementing their victory in 1991. Known as 'the Wallabies', they were arguably at their best in the mid 80s when players like Michael Lynagh and David Campese came to the fore. However, a new generation of players like George Gregan and John Eales helped to lead them to that second World Cup triumph as well as back-to-back Tri Nations victories.

Times have been a little harder on them since that golden age. Australia were eliminated by England in the quarter-finals of the 2007 World Cup, a seismic shock given how weak the English were supposed to be, and they haven't won the Tri Nations since 2001. Never write them off, though, they're bound to be back in greater strength soon.

South Africa

The Springboks were only readmitted to international rugby in 1992 after the end of apartheid, but in that short time they've managed to assert their strength quite effectively in international competition. Winners of the World Cup in 1995, as we've discussed already, they also prevented England from winning back-to-back trophies, by winning it again in 2007.

A physically strong and well-organised team, they play their home games across the nation to ensure that everyone gets a chance to see them. However, their spiritual home is Ellis Park in Johannesburg, the scene of that gripping and poignant 1995 triumph.

The British & Irish Lions

The greatest honour for a British or Irish rugby player, perhaps even greater than representing their national team, is to be chosen to play for the Lions. The British & Irish Lions, to give them their full name, are a super-team chosen to play in special tours. They don't play in World Cups or club competitions, but they are an invading army who sweep into one country and battle out a long run of matches against club sides, building up to a short series of ultra-serious games, called Test matches, against the national side. Alternatively, they are a misbegotten, poorly organised, ragtag bunch of wannabe superstars who rock up in someone else's nation and get repeatedly walloped until they give up their delusions of grandeur and slink home with their tails between their legs. It really depends on who you ask and when you ask them. Other nations take as much pride in beating the Lions as UK players take in representing them.

A combined British and Irish side had been touring the Southern Hemisphere since 1888 in various guises, few of which ever earned official backing. It wasn't until 1910 that the four rugby organisations finally came together under one billing, but the 'Lions' name didn't stick until 1924, when a journalist began to refer to them after the animal that adorned their badge. See, that's how corporate branding should work. No focus groups, no consultants, just something naturally snappy. It's certainly got more of a natural snappiness than the Rotherham Titans, hasn't it?

It might be difficult for football fans to get their heads around the concept of a team set up specifically to play one-off games, but it's important to remember that international rugby was built on tours. With no World Cup until 1987, tours were how nations judged themselves. The Lions were the medium for hemispheres to judge themselves. Their games, essentially, were the World Cups and then there's that word again. Pride.

There is no national anthem for a Lions side to swell with pride at, although, with toe-curling inevitability, someone did once try to contrive one in 2005. The players are expected to recognise that they are the best of the best, and they invariably do. The competition within the squad is legendary. When a group of players, some with egos the size of a house, come together, it's difficult to insist that everyone gets along, especially if they've only just finished fighting each other in the Six Nations. The best Lions teams, however, are the ones who can quickly put their differences aside and fight for each other on the pitch. Still, ex-players have said that training sessions could be just as intense as actual matches as the players do their best to secure a place in the Test match starting line-up.

Because the Lions tour so infrequently, usually every four years, there is intense media speculation and coverage of everything they do. Even the announcement of the squad is a major news event and the choice of a captain and coach can be debated for weeks afterwards. The Lions are representative of so many clubs, nations and organisations that there is great pressure on them to perform and the treatment of those teams who do not deliver can be savage.

In 2005, Sir Clive Woodward took the Lions to New Zealand. Woodward had just won the World Cup with England and had built an enormous backroom staff of 'experts', including the New Labour spin doctor Alistair Campbell. Despite his specially commissioned anthem, his towering reputation for organisation and one of the strongest touring squads in years, England were whitewashed, losing all three Test matches. They returned to the UK in near-disgrace.

The fallout was so severe that Woodward actually left rugby to work in football for a brief and equally unsuccessful period.

Some Lions stories are so magnificent that they become legendary, but before you can truly tell the tale of Call 99 and the Battle of Boet Erasmus, it's important to set the scene. Back in 1974, when something shocking happened, there weren't TV cameras all over the stadium providing experts with every angle they needed to dissect it. There weren't bitter recriminations from the authorities afterwards because even the people involved only had the vaguest of ideas of what had just happened. It was a simpler time and there were ... erm ... simpler methods to alter the balance of games.

As well as being one of the best, South Africa were also one of the most physical teams in the world. Touring teams tended to leave with more bruises than victories, but all that would change with the arrival of the 1974 Lions. With the spine of one of the greatest Welsh teams of all time and led by the Irishman Willie John McBride, they came with the intention of finally bringing down the Southern Hemisphere giants. The only problem was that the South Africans were not entirely keen on allowing that to happen. The Lions were battered by the opponents, always off the ball and always behind the back of the referee. Studs were raised in rucks, punches were thrown in mauls and still there were no recriminations.

It was McBride who came up with the idea of 'Call 99', a simple code to announce that the Lions were getting their retaliation in first. At the sound of the call every Lion was under strict instructions to run to his nearest opponent and hit him very hard in the face. Seriously.

Full participation was mandatory. McBride's theory was that, with every single red-shirted player throwing punches, the referee wouldn't be able to take any action. He couldn't send everybody off, could he? It worked too. Even JPR Williams, down the other end of the pitch at the time of the call, ran the best part of 60 yards to lamp the first Springbok to get in his way. Chaos broke out across the pitch as skirmishes developed everywhere you looked. Rugby players being rugby players, it wasn't a case of anyone winning or losing the fight. Every time they got knocked down, they jumped back up again for more.

The Lions won 26-9, eventually winning the series 3-0. JPR Williams later said that he felt quite bad about what had happened. In an interview with *The Guardian* in 2006, he said that, many years later on a train, he had unknowingly met the man he'd walloped.

'We had a lovely chat,' he said. 'When I got home I looked in the match programme and saw that it was the guy I had punched. He never mentioned it during the whole time we were talking. What a gentleman!'

Ladies and gentlemen, I give you rugby union.

The Barbarians

One of the most glorious hangovers from the old days of rugby is the continued existence of the Barbarians, an invitational club where individual quality is vital, but is not as important as class and dignity. The Barbarians, or the 'Baa-Baas' as they are occasionally known, are the most Corinthian of clubs, as their club motto explains.

'Rugby Football is a game for gentlemen of all classes, but for no bad sportsmen in any class.'

They were brought into being by one William Percy Carpmael in 1890. To call Carpmael a big fan of rugby was perhaps to do him a disservice. It wasn't so much the game that he believed in, as the ethos that surrounded it: the camaraderie, the culture, the spirit and the standards. He wanted a team where winning was simply not as important as the way you conducted yourself in life.

The Barbarians are honour-bound to only play the most attractive of rugby. It is frowned upon to be caught playing percentages, rucking and mauling the ball over the line. Even kicking the ball for goal is an offence, especially if it's from a distance. That's simply not the way to conduct yourself when such high standards have been set. Barbarians are obliged to get the ball out, get it out quickly and then get at the opposition, as they did in 1973 when they scored what is widely believed to be the greatest try of all time against New Zealand, the one I was telling you about earlier. Even now, it is referred to simply as 'That Try'.

The Barbarians have no home stadium and do not play in any competitions, club or international. They play invitational one-off matches, or the Final Challenge against foreign touring sides. Any player from any nation can represent them. They invite players based on their skill, but also on their behaviour on and off the field. There are Australians, New Zealanders, Canadians and Italians, players from every country, but there are no cheats and no undesirable types.

You can easily recognise the Barbarians from their black and white hooped kit, but keep an eye on their socks. They're the only team who allow their players to wear their club socks when they represent the team. Even though the long tours that sustained the game have all but disappeared with the advent of professionalism, the Barbarians still live on and there's something strangely comforting about that.

The Brumbies

Formed in 1996 as a third Australian franchise for the big-money southern hemisphere Super 14 league, very little was actually expected of the Brumbies. Made up of rejects from the New South Wales Waratahs and the Queensland Reds, people thought that they were just there to make up the numbers. Big mistake. Players like scrum-half George Gregan and centre Stirling Mortlock made a mockery of expert opinion and carried the Brumbies to a number of memorable triumphs. Winners of the Super 14 (formerly the Super 12) in both 2001 and 2004, the Canberra-based side have provided a string of players for the national team.

Their history actually predates the post-professional Super 14. Formerly known as the ACT (Australian Capital Territory) Brumbies, they were a renowned club with a history that dates back to 1938. The Brumbies beat tourists Tonga in 1973 before their greatest triumph, a victory over the mighty Welsh side in 1978.

Incidentally, a 'Brumby' is the Australian name for a wild horse. There are thousands of them scattered across Australia, descendants of lost or escaped horses from the early days of European colonisation. So there you go.

The Crusaders

The most successful team in the history of the Super 14 are the Crusaders, based in Canterbury, New Zealand. Not that you'd have known that after the first season of the competition, when they finished dead last. A complete overhaul of the team was ordered and progress was swift. In 1998, despite losing three of their first four games, the Crusaders won their first title. It wasn't to be their last.

Further success followed in 1999, 2000, 2002, 2005, 2006 and 2008. Led by inspirational captain Todd Blackadder, who took over as coach in 2009, they dominated the competition as well as hogging the places in the national team. When New Zealand trotted out against Ireland in 2002, all but one of the starting line-up were Crusaders.

Leicester

Comfortably the most successful club side in post-professional English club rugby, not only have Leicester never been relegated from the Premiership, but they've never even finished outside of the top six. With four consecutive league wins between 1999 and 2002, they've struck fear into the hearts of their opponents for over a decade. Their success isn't limited to England either. As well as all of those domestic trophies, they're the only team to have won the Heineken Cup in back-to-back seasons. Leicester's players were led through that period of unparalled success by skipper Martin Johnson, also England captain and gigantic man-mountain.

Leicester have been in existence since 1880 when they were the product of a three-way merger of local club sides. From a relatively ignominious opening in amateur rugby, they blossomed just before the arrival of professionalism with their ABC Club, led by Graham Rowntree, attracting particular attention. The ABC reference, incidentally, came from the fact that Leicester players wore letters on their backs instead of numbers.

Leicester have improved so much in the last decade that they now hold the distinction of owning the largest club rugby stadium in the UK, a 23,500 capacity arena.

Llanelli

Back in the days when a touring side would make a point of taking on the region's strongest clubs, you could get some pretty strange match-ups. International players, blooded and bonded over a long journey, would roll into town, draw breath and then obliterate the pride of the community, before moving on to do the same thing to someone else. For a club side to beat an international side was difficult. For a club side like Llanelli to beat the 1972 All Blacks, well that was just inconceivable.

Even Llanelli's early score didn't alter the pre-match perception. Roy Bergier bravely charged down a kick and then leapt on the loose ball to claim the try, which was converted by Phil Bennett. Normality seemed to be resumed when New Zealand brought the score to 6-3 with a penalty, but that was their only success. Instead of capitulating to the inevitable, the Welsh side rose up and fought even harder.

The All Blacks were a huge side, strong and physical, but Llanelli were inspired and matched them all the way and when Andy Hill struck a long-range penalty home to make it 9-3, it was clear that something extraordinary was happening. For all of New Zealand's ferocity, they couldn't get back into the game.

At full time, the Llanelli players were lifted into the air by the supporters who charged on to the pitch to celebrate. Coach Carwyn Jones had led the British & Irish Lions to a series win over the Kiwis, but this was far more of a surprise. The celebrations went on long into the night, with so many people getting involved that they drank every pub in the locality dry. Beating the All Blacks will make a man thirsty, you see.

Important information for new fans

Local clubs

If you want to know more about the game of rugby union, the best thing you can do is head to your local rugby club. Most of them will show important games in their clubhouse and you'll find no shortage of people to welcome you with open arms.

This isn't to say that every club has a willing assistant on hand to talk you through the Experimental Law Variations of 2008 or the slow evolution of the Courage Leagues through the 1980s. Only that you're far more likely to get a polite response to the question 'I don't get it, who was offside?' than you are anywhere else with any other sport.

Brilliantly, most local clubs are like Masonic lodges, so if you really like it and you fit in, you can expect to make lots of new friends from a wide variety of backgrounds. Rugby draws a broad church of followers and it's not unusual to have a club made up of plumbers and policemen, taxi drivers and taxidermists. Well, alright, taxidermists are pretty rare, but you get the point.

Drinking

Good, solid drinking is as essential to the game of rugby union as good, solid shoes are to the game of golf. Because rugby fans can be trusted to last 80 minutes without having to clamber over the stadium walls to hit the opposing fans with heavy things, alcohol is freely available before, during and after the game. It's not quite mandatory that you drink while you watch, but sometimes you wonder. If certain key members of the rugby fraternity ever managed to find themselves in a position of power, you wouldn't want to rule it out.

There are a number of magnificent pubs on the walk from the train station to Twickenham Stadium and, if you time your journey right, you should have a chance to pop in at several of them before kick-off time approaches. There are no 'home' pubs in this sport because the fans don't need to be segregated from each other. You can sit in the beer gardens with the opposing fans without any fear of reprisals, which is a good thing, because the chances are that you'll be sat next to them in the stadium as well.

Mixing

Rugby crowds are self-policing and this applies to anything from violence to antisocial behaviour. A friend of my dad's once went to watch his team, Saracens, playing away at Rosslyn Park and sat with the home fans. Tired of having a giant red and white flag waved in his face by the youths in front of him, he politely asked if they could put it down so that he could actually watch the match. They ignored him and continued to wave it back and forth. A little firmer this time, he asked if they were going to put it down, or if he would have to put it down for them.

'Oh yeah?' one of the youths sneered at him. 'You and whose army?'

'Him and us,' growled an entire row of Rosslyn Park fans behind them. The flag couldn't have hit the floor any quicker had it been weighted down with the Saracens' front row.

This kind of thing, heart-warming as it may be, is incredibly rare. Not for the fact that you can't always count on a friendly Rosslyn Park crowd, but because you wouldn't be put in that position anyway. Rugby fans, even during moments of tension, tend not to do anything to upset anyone else. Unless you count singing 'Bread of Heaven' at the top of your voice as upsetting.

I was at Twickenham in 2001 for the Tetley Bitter Cup Final between Newcastle and Harlequins. The fans were scattered willy-nilly across the stadium in little pockets of friends and family with no thought given to segregation. It was a tight game that went the distance, eventually ending 30-27 with Newcastle scoring their crucial points in injury time by a very debatable try. If that had been a football match, the authorities would have just bolted the doors, nailed a roof on the stadium and come back in five years on the off chance that anyone had survived. With rugby, it wasn't a problem. Handshakes all round, a bit of boozy banter and off home. Via the pub. My kind of sport.

You don't boo the other team's kicker, you don't hurl abuse at the players, you don't boo the national anthem. You just enjoy the game and have a good singsong.

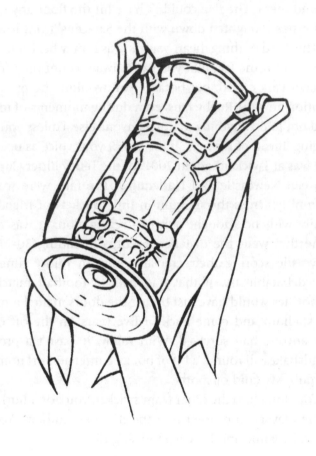

Final word

So there it is. You now know how rugby union works and where it all came from. Keep this book close and you may even have a better understanding of the rules than people who have been playing it for years. You know the great players and the teams that they played in. You know the competitions and what they all mean, and you know a little about what happens at a live game.

Rugby is a sport that has shackled itself with complicated laws and is still paying the price for having been organised by people who had a vested interest in ensuring that common people didn't play it. Dig a little deeper, work a little harder, and you'll find what they were trying so desperately to protect. A sport that may not have the glamour of modern football, or the grace of cricket, but that offers something different and something well worthy of respect in its own right. Rugby is an exhilarating physical contest, a merging of brains and brawn and a clash of pace against power. It's fun, it's entertaining and it's getting bigger all the time.

Enjoy.

Glossary

22-metre drop-out If an attacking team punts the ball upfield and it crosses over the goal-line, a defender can touch the ball down and remove any pressure. He can then wander to his own 22-yard line and restart play with a drop kick.

22-yard line The line that runs across the pitch, 22 yards away from the goal-line. A kick from inside here will lead to a line-out wherever the ball leaves the pitch.

Amateurism Erstwhile defining tenet of rugby union. Up until 1995, it was illegal to pay players. Even the international players were essentially ordinary chaps enjoying their hobby.

Anglo–Welsh Cup A tournament contested by teams from England and Wales.

Backs The name given to the quicker, lighter players who make up the back-line. Backs come in several varieties including wingers, centres, fly-halves and the obligatory full-back.

The Barbarians An invitational super-team who play friendlies and exhibition games around the world. The Barbarians were established with the intention of upholding the Corinthian values of the sport.

Bind The grip of one player to an opposing player in the scrum. A good bind is on the shirt of the opposite number. A bad one is on his ears, or his arm, or his collar, or anything like that. That's just not nice.

Blindside flanker The man on the third row of the scrum, on the side nearest to the sideline.

Blood replacement At the first sign of blood, the injured player must leave the pitch to be patched up. He can be replaced by a substitute, but it won't count against the number of substitutes allowed. It's purely a temporary measure to encourage good health and safety.

'Bread of Heaven' Traditional Welsh rugby song. Always performed with great gusto.

Breakdown When a player is tackled and falls to the floor, it is known as the 'breakdown'. A player who is quickly on the scene to the ruck that develops is known as being 'quick to the breakdown'.

The British & Irish Lions A super-team made up of the very best players from England, Scotland, Ireland and Wales. The Lions are selected every four years to tour a Southern Hemisphere nation; being chosen to play for them is even more of an honour than playing for your country.

Calcutta Cup The competition within a competition, the trophy awarded to the winner of the England v Scotland game in every Six Nations.

Celtic League The super league that includes teams from Scotland, Ireland and Wales.

Centres Centres come in two flavours, inside centres and outside centres. They are also referred to as 'the midfield'.

Challenge Cup The secondary European tournament for teams not quite good enough to qualify for the European Cup.

The Championship The second flight of English rugby, lurking underneath the Premiership.

Conversion Every try leads to a conversion attempt from any point in line with where the ball went down. A successful conversion, i.e. sending the ball through the middle of the posts and over the crossbar, is worth 2 points.

Driving maul A maul that pushes forwards towards the try-line.

Drop goal A drop kick from open play that passes above the crossbar and between the posts. Drop goals are very hard to score, not least because the ball actually has to touch the ground before it can be kicked. And you've seen the shape of that ball.

European Cup The major European tournament and arguably the ultimate prize in club rugby. Fiercely competitive, with teams from France, England, Ireland, Wales and Scotland all fighting through pool stages and knockout rounds to a one-off, make-or-break final.

Experimental Law Variations (ELVs) The experimental rule changes of 2008. Rugby's powerbrokers are never happy and are constantly trying to find ways to improve the game. In 2008, they changed a whole swathe of rules, confusing coaches up and down the land and making the construction of this book even more difficult than it should have been. Every effort has been made to make sure that only the retained ELVs are included.

Five-metre scrum No scrum can be held closer to the line than five metres. If they could be held closer, all you'd get would be teams trying to steal a few inches here and there and attempting to score tries with just one push. It wouldn't be very dignified at all, would it?

Five Nations The former name given to the Six Nations. Before 2000, it was contested only by France, England, Scotland, Ireland and Wales.

Fly-half The foremost of the backs and usually the designated kicker.

Forwards The name given to the bigger, harder players who make up the scrum. Forwards come in several varieties including props, hookers, locks, flankers and the number eight.

Full-back The poor chap at the back of the backs. Usually responsible for catching those hellish lofted balls and almost always the last line of the defence.

Garryowen A lofted kick that stays in play. If you punt the ball up in the air and you all chase after it, it's a Garryowen.

Goal-Line (*see* Try-Line)

Goals Those big H-shaped things at either end of the pitch. Come on, you knew that, didn't you?

Gone against the head When a scrum is won by the team who didn't have the put-in.

Grubber kick A hard kick where the ball bounces along the ground.

Home Nations The name given to the Five/Six Nations prior to 1910. Before then it was contested only by England, Scotland, Ireland and Wales.

Hooker The chap in the middle of the front row of the scrum. He also throws the ball in at line-outs.

International Rugby Board (IRB) The ultimate ruling body of the global game.

Kick-off The start of the game.

Knock-on The ball can't be passed forwards, even if you're passing to yourself. If you try to catch the ball, but you flap at it and divert it forwards, it's a knock on. Which is a foul. It's not a knock on if you catch it before it hits the ground, nor is it a knock on if you charge down a kick. Only if you go to catch it, fumble it and it lands on the ground is it considered to be a knock on.

Line-out The method used to restart the game when the ball has left the field of play over the side touchlines. The team who didn't touch the ball last (except for penalties) get to throw the ball in between two lines of players who will jump up in the air and try to grab it in mid-flight. It's very exciting to watch.

Locks The secondrow forwards behind the front row. Usually very, very tall.

Loosehead prop The prop on the left-hand side of the front row.

Mark If a player is attempting to catch a ball approaching him from a great height he can ward off potential predators by shouting out 'MARK!' This indicates to the referee that he is going to catch the ball and then kick it back up the pitch and no one is allowed to stop him doing it. The mark can only be called within the defending team's 22-yard line.

Maul Like a ruck, but when the player stays on his feet. If other players can be quick to the scene, they can force the ball forwards by pushing against the other team's pack. It is possible to form a maul and then force the ball all the way over the try-line, although as soon as the maul holds up, they must release the ball or lose possession completely.

National League The division below the Premiership for the other club sides in England.

Number eight The man at the rear of the scrum.

Obstruction Standing in front of a player and blocking his progress, whether he has the ball or not. It's not on.

Offside The ball carrier has to be the furthest forward of the team. Anyone interfering with the game who is further forward than that will be penalised. Offside also covers offences around scrums, line-outs, rucks and mauls.

Openside flanker The man on the third row of the scrum furthest from the sideline.

Pass The act of giving the ball to a team-mate. The ball can never be passed forwards, only sideways or backwards.

Penalty The punishment for a deliberate offence. The captain will choose from four options:
1. A kick at goal, worth 3 points.
2. A scrum with the put-in.
3. A tap penalty that restarts the game quickly.
4. The chance to kick the ball out of touch and win the line-out to restart play.

Penalty try If a referee believes that a foul has been committed with the intention of stopping a try from being scored, he can award a penalty try. Unlike in football, this isn't a chance to score some points, it *is* some points. The referee simply assumes that, as you were going to score anyway, he may as well just give you the points.

Phase rugby After every breakdown, assuming that the team in possession retain the ball, it is a new phase of play. Therefore, if you have the ball and there's a ruck, which you win, it will be the second phase. Another ruck and another retention is another phase, a third in this case. Phases keep increasing until the team lose possession.

Pool The name given to a group of teams in a tournament.

Premiership The top division of English club rugby.

Prop A prop forward. The enormous blokes on either side of the hooker at the front of the scrum.

Put-in The team whose scrum-half puts the ball in are said to have the 'put-in'. This means that it is far more likely that they will win the scrum.

Red card A last resort used by the referee to permanently remove a player from the field of play.

Referee The man in charge of the game with the power to send players off for a ten-minute period, or even permanently.

Rolling maul A maul that pushes forwards, but where the ball is repositioned along its axis. A risky way to hold possession.

Ruck When a player is tackled and falls to the ground, a ruck will develop. This is where more than three players contest for possession of the ball by, very basically, pushing against each other until the ball is safely behind them. There's a lot more to it than that, but that's why there are two whole sections devoted to it.

Rugby Football Union (RFU) The governing body of English rugby union.

Rugby league The other kind of rugby, popular in the north of England. Rugby league was created after the schism of 1895 split the sport in two. Rugby union, the one that you've just read about, stayed amateur until 1995. Rugby league went professional straight away.

Scrum A way of restarting a game after an accidental infringement, or as a team's choice of medium for a penalty. The two packs crouch, touch and engage and then attempt to wrest control of the ball from each other, either pushing forwards with it, or passing it out to the backs.

Scrum-half The man responsible for linking up the backs with the forwards and putting the ball in the scrum.

Second-row forwards (*see* Locks)

Sideline The line running along the side of the pitch marking the boundaries of play.

Sin bin Where yellow-carded rugby players go to think about what they've done. Every cautioned player must spend ten minutes in the sin bin before he's allowed back on to the pitch.

Six Nations The annual international round-robin tournament contested by England, France, Ireland, Scotland, Italy and Wales.

Spear tackle Picking up a man and throwing him headfirst into the ground is a spear tackle. It's also incredibly dangerous as a neck is very rarely as solid as the earth's surface.

Substitutes Spare players who can come on to the pitch to replace underperforming or injured colleagues.

Tackle An attempt to stop an opponent with physical force. Tackles must be below the shoulders and must be made with the arms. You can't barge, you can't trip and you can't grab anyone round the head or the neck. It's a violent game, but it's not that violent.

Tap penalty Not all penalties need to be kicked. Instead of punting for goal or taking the scrum, a captain can decide to get the ball back in open play instantly by tapping the ball with his foot into his arms and then running.

Test A clash between the international sides of two nations. Thought to derive from generic conversations about 'England testing their strength against Australia,' as opposed to it being some kind of practice game.

Touchline (*see* Sideline)

Tighthead prop The prop on the right-hand side of the front row of the scrum.

Touch judges The referee's assistants, seen on the flanks of the pitch or behind the goals at kick attempts, waving their flags if the ball passes between the posts.

Tour With no international competitions, and very few actual competitions, rugby teams used to test each other by going on tour. Some teams still exist purely for that purpose, like the British & Irish Lions and, to a lesser extent, the Barbarians. In these professional times, tours have been phased out and replaced by competitions, but they still exist to a lesser degree.

Tri Nations The annual three-way tournament contested by South Africa, New Zealand and Australia.

Try The act of putting the ball down over the goal-line. A try is worth five points and will lead to a conversion attempt.

Try-line The line that everyone is trying to cross with the ball in their hands. Put the ball down behind this and you've scored five points.

William Webb Ellis The legend behind the invention of rugby. Apparently, Webb Ellis grabbed a football off the ground in the middle of a match and ran off with it. That's fighting talk where I come from. It probably didn't happen anyway, according to historians. It didn't stop the rugby authorities naming the World Cup after him, though.

Wingers The very quick backs on either end of the back-line. You get right-wingers and left-wingers.

World Cup The ultimate test for any international team, held once every four years since 1987, in 2007, 2011, 2015 etc.

Yellow card A disciplinary measure used to remove misbehaving players from the pitch for a period of ten minutes. Useful for allowing angry players to regain their composure, or even to punish a team for persistent fouling by, say, sending the next one to offend straight to the sin bin.

Index

Also available:

Everything You Ever Wanted to
Know About Golf But Were
too Afraid to Ask

ISBN: 9781408114971

Everything You Ever Wanted to
Know About Cricket But Were
too Afraid to Ask

ISBN: 9781408114957

Everything You Ever Wanted to
Know About Football But Were
too Afraid to Ask

ISBN: 9781408114964

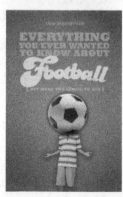